UNIVERSITY OF LIVERPOOL

013508431

KU-084-366

LIVERPOOL HOPE UNIVERSITY
THE SHEPPARD - WORLOCK LIBRARY

91

1991

99

GROUP WORK IN SECONDARY SCHOOLS

Other books by BARRINGTON KAYE

The Development of the Architectural Profession in Britain
  (Allen and Unwin, London)

Natten hade varit Mild och Öm
  (Almqvist & Wiksell/Gebers, Stockholm)

Upper Nankin Street, Singapore
  (University of Malaya Press, Singapore; distributed by Oxford
  University Press)

Bringing Up Children in Ghana
  (Allen and Unwin, London)

GROUP WORK IN SECONDARY SCHOOLS
and the training of teachers in its methods

'Everybody wants to know more, don't they?'
  15-year-old schoolboy

BARRINGTON KAYE
AND
IRVING ROGERS

1968   OXFORD UNIVERSITY PRESS

Oxford University Press, Ely House, London W.1

GLASGOW NEW YORK TORONTO MELBOURNE WELLINGTON
CAPE TOWN SALISBURY IBADAN NAIROBI LUSAKA ADDIS ABABA
BOMBAY CALCUTTA MADRAS KARACHI LAHORE DACCA
KUALA LUMPUR HONG KONG TOKYO

© *Barrington Kaye and Irving Rogers 1968*

E94462
371.3

PRINTED IN GREAT BRITAIN BY
NORTHUMBERLAND PRESS LIMITED, GATESHEAD

From: B K, I R. *To:* K A, E C B,
GCB, UD, AF, JAH, JDH, NMH,
MHM, DMP, KER, AW, LW, NW

Preface

In offering this introduction to group work as a teaching method for secondary schools we should like to emphasize that it is not our intention to suggest that group work should replace existing, teacher-directed methods, or that it is a method which is necessarily suitable for all subjects, all ages and all schools. It is our view that the teaching needs of children vary from time to time in relation to a large number of variables. The needs of the subject or topic being taught, the composition of the class, the range of abilities within it, the previous experience of the children and of the teacher, are only some of the factors which should be considered.

The raising of the school-leaving age, the recommendations of the Newsom Report, the provisions of Mode III entry to the C.S.E. examination, the Nuffield schemes and the present continuing discussion of the pros and cons of non-streamed classes are all reasons why, at the present time, secondary teachers are taking another look at the range of teaching methods available to them. Team teaching, group work, inter-disciplinary inquiry, discussion methods, school or year projects—these and many other approaches are available to teachers as well as the more traditional class-teaching methods. One of the reasons, we suspect, why they are not put to greater use is that there are not readily available in this country suggestions as to how these more informal methods can be implemented in classes used to traditional teacher-directed lessons. This is not to say, of course, that there do not exist many books presenting good arguments supporting such approaches. Indeed, it would no doubt be possible to find passages justifying the kind of methods we have in mind in most of the writings of educational theorists, from the ancient Greeks onwards. But what have been lacking, we feel, are fairly detailed, down-to-earth handbooks, making specific suggestions about how to organize and conduct such teaching methods in normal secondary school classes. It is the aim of the present volume to fill this gap with regard to one method in particular—that of group work. But we should like to stress that, in taking this particular approach, we are not arguing thereby that group work should be universally adopted as the only method to be followed. On the other hand, we do think that it is a method which should be in every teacher's repertoire, so that when the circumstances justify its adoption, he or she is not inhibited from using it simply from ignorance of its basic procedures.[1]

Our second concern—and it is one that follows logically from what we have said above—is with the problem of training student teachers in group-work methods. As it would appear that the college at which the authors have been working is one of the few in this country that specifically trains secondary students in such methods, we have ventured to include in our discussions some of the ways in which we have set about this task, in the hope that they may be of interest to others concerned with the training of teachers.

We should like to take this opportunity of thanking those of our colleagues, both teachers and tutors, who have given us their advice and comments, and in particular Tom Evans of Gordano School and Anthony Weaver of Redland College, both of whom have read the book in typescript and made many detailed and helpful comments and suggestions. Neither, however, should be held responsible for any omissions or shortcomings which remain.

---

[1] We should like to draw attention to a book, published in the United States, dealing with the same subject, to which we should like to think this volume is complementary: *Group Work in Education* by Ruth Strang (New York, Harper, 3rd edition, 1958); and also to the work of H.A. Thelen in *Dynamics of Groups at Work* (University of Chicago Press, (1954), and in *Education and the Human Quest* (Harper & Row, 1960).

Our thanks are due to the following, for permission to quote from the works cited:

Penguins Books Ltd. (p. 77); Anna Freud, the Hogarth Press Ltd. and the International Universities Press Ltd. (p. 79); Basic Books Inc. (p. 82).

Finally, we should like to record our gratitude to our colleagues at Redland College, Bristol, for their support; to the heads and teachers of the schools in Bristol and Somerset without whose co-operation the experiments described in this book would not have been possible; to our students, whose enthusiastic response to our suggestions has been our chief reward; and last but not least, to the children themselves who, we hope, have not only enjoyed this new approach to learning but also benefited from it.

Bristol and Portishead, 1967.

Contents

1. CHILDREN'S REACTIONS   1

2. AN EXPERIMENT IN THE TRAINING OF
TEACHERS   12
   The tradition of secondary teaching method   12
   *The sources of a change in attitude towards subject
   teaching*   14
   Implications for the training of teachers   17
   A large-scale training programme   19

3. THE NATURE OF GROUP WORK   26
   Distinction between group work and group teaching   26
   A working definition of group work   30
   The teacher's role   31

4. THE ORGANIZATION OF GROUP WORK   37
   The time available   37
   The specification of the work: content   38
   The specification of the work: sources   41
   Different approaches to group work   44
   The formation of the groups: sociometry   47
   Problems in forming groups   48
   The group procedure   53

The availability of materials and facilities   56
The evaluation of progress   57
Provision for reporting back   59

5. GROUP WORK IN ACTION   61
Introducing the method: a development of co-operative working   61
Thematic group work: an outline of a working scheme   65
The effects of group work on pupils' social behaviour   68
Group work and examinations   69

6. THE RATIONALE OF GROUP WORK   75
The psychology of puberty and adolescence   75
The psychology of mental development   80
Discipline versus self-direction   83
The Lippitt and White experiments   88
The Deutsch experiments   94
Other experimental evidence   96

7. TRAINING TEACHERS IN GROUP-WORK METHODS   101
Difficulties to be overcome   101
The student's need of prior self-confidence in a formal teaching situation   102
The need for personal experience of group work   104
The relation of the student's own experience to the organization of group work   106
The timing of suggestions for the organization of group work   107
The organization of a course on group work   109

8. CONCLUSIONS   115
   Group work not a universal teaching method   115
   Group work and 'discipline'   116
   Organization and the teacher's role   118

APPENDIX   123

REFERENCES AND BOOKS FOR FURTHER
READING   132

INDEX   137

1 Children's reactions

'We sent away to firms, British Petroleum, and Shell and places like that, and got information from the pamphlets they sent to us, and we worked on that.'

'We did a model of a reactor in a boiler.'

'We did a project on how coal is used in power stations, and we sent away for information, and we visited the Portishead Power Station, and also we did an experiment to see how much actually goes into the power station. We all found it very interesting, and it's quite amazing how coal helps to get the electricity out over the country.'

'So you actually performed the experiment as part of your work?'

'Yes, instead of making a model of it.'

'We've been doing electricity, the use of electricity, with information from pamphlets and books we got from the library.'

'And did you do an experiment?'

'No, we made a model, to find out where the electricity goes to.'

'We're doing nuclear power.'

'Where did you get your information from?'

'The Atomic Energy Authority of London.'

'And did you write the letters?'

'Yes, we all wrote away.'

'The teacher didn't write the letters?'

'Oh, no!'

This excerpt is from a conversation between one of the authors and the members of a class of fourteen-year-old children in a Bristol school who had spent a term studying the production of power in Britain, under the guidance of two student teachers. Instead of being taught as a whole class, the children had been working in five groups, and each group had pursued a separate topic, reporting back to the whole class their findings at the end of term. The groups had been formed on the basis of the children's choice of topic. Each group had made its own plan of work, decided on how best to present its results (by models, by demonstrations, by charts and illustrations), and allocated among the group members the various tasks involved, with the guidance of the teacher.

The two student teachers in charge of the class were under the supervision of the class teacher and of a visiting college tutor. Their concern was to give the children a framework within which they could have freedom to pursue their investigation. After a preliminary talk in which the idea of group work was explained and various topics discussed, the children formed themselves into groups and thereafter each group worked by itself, until the final stage of reporting back. The students and the class teacher visited each group to watch progress and to give advice and guidance where needed. At one stage it became evident that help was needed generally on the theory and construction of generators, and the teacher gave a lesson to the whole class on the subject. Two films dealing with different aspects of power production were shown to the whole class at appropriate stages during the work. Apart from these occasions, the children worked together in their groups.

Within each group the various tasks were allocated by common agreement: one child wrote a letter of inquiry to one firm, a second child to another, a third did the necessary research in the library, while two others made a preliminary design for the model. There was constant interchange of ideas and roles so that the final work that was produced—whether model, report or demonstration—was a joint production, and could not be said to be the work of any one child. At the end of the term, the supervising college tutor asked the children how they felt about this aspect of group work.

'The thing which is often said about working this way is that you work together with other people instead of on your own as an individual. Have any of you found this an advantage or a disadvantage, or would you prefer to go ahead on your own, as a member of a class being taught, than as a group?'

'I think it's an advantage. You can sort out the problems, really, and find out things quicker with more people.'

'With atomic energy it's very hard for one person to find it all out and we've got four, which is much easier, because we can muck in together. We find it much easier.'
'There's a lot I didn't know about atoms that I know now.'

'Mucking in together' is in fact the essential characteristic of group work. The work is planned jointly and carried out jointly. In this way each member of the group is responsible to his fellows for his own contribution; he has to satisfy them as to its accuracy and presentation. In turn, he is critic and judge of their contribution. It might be argued that although group work appears to give children freedom to pursue their own interests, in fact each individual child is constrained by the wishes of the majority. The tutor asked the members of different groups in another class about this. The children had been studying the development of law and order.

'What was your group doing?'
'We were doing quarter sessions, and all the different sessions they have for cases.'
'The different kinds of courts?'
'Yes.'
'Did you find it interesting?'
'Yes. We were doing a play on the procedure when the crime is committed.'
'I see. You were in fact acting in your group, were you?'
'Yes.'
'And what about your group?'
'Our group started off doing Saxon and Ancient Law. We learnt something about it, and then after that we started on a play.'
'And yours?'
'We were doing the medieval times, the law and order of medieval times, the crimes that were committed, and the kind of courts there were, and the first parliament.'
'And what about your group?'
'We started off from the beginning of the police force as we know it now—you know, from the constables and the watch—and went all the way through to the police force as we know it today.'
'Who chose these topics—the headings that you were going to do?'

'The students.'

'I see. So how much freedom have you had in fact, to do what you wanted to do?'

'Oh, we had freedom, because if we didn't like it we could always have gone into another group.'

'But what about within the group itself?'

'Well, we discussed it first, you know, and then had a majority vote for it.'

'But what about when you were actually working? How much freedom did you have to follow up the line that perhaps you were interested in?'

'Well, it was according to the group.'

'So it was a group decision and you were free if you wanted to take it further?'

'Well, if you wanted to do more research, then you could do it, but usually we just find out something, jot it down in our books, you know, and memorize it and talk about it.'

'Freedom' is a key word in group work. It is also a highly emotive word, and it is important to be clear about the kind of freedom that group work offers to the children engaged in it. It certainly does not mean freedom for pupils to do just what they like, when they like and how they like. In fact, unless they have been brought up with very much greater responsibility for their own self-direction than is the case with the vast majority of ordinary children, this kind of complete freedom is not freedom at all; it exposes children to the tyranny of passing emotions, and gives rise to a sense of insecurity which may even lead to desperate action. Too many educational reformers, justifiably appalled by the close direction and petty restrictions of the traditional classroom, have fled to the opposite extreme and tried to allow children greater responsibility for themselves than they are able to cope with. Children need the security afforded by a framework for their actions; they also need freedom to manipulate within that framework. Group work gives them this latter freedom. The general direction of the work, the field of subject matter to be dealt with, and some indication of the topics to be covered, are all usually given by the teacher. These may well arise out of discussion with the class, and the teacher will look for and adopt suggestions from the pupils; but it is upon the teacher's authority, and therefore upon his responsibility, that the overall plan depends.

This is particularly the case with classes unused to group work or other informal methods. In such classes, to give children too much responsibility for their own programme of work at the outset simply leads to anxiety and consequent disorder. Being used to having all their decisions made for them by the teacher they are unable to accept suddenly too heavy a load of responsibility. They must be led to greater freedom of choice by stages and in the first stage they depend very much upon a framework provided by the teacher, within which they can make their own choices and pursue their own plans. From the confidence which success at this stage brings they will then be prepared to accept greater responsibility next time and, of course, the teacher will then be more prepared to give it to them.

Having decided upon the plan and the various topics the teacher may then go on to draw up what may be called the specification of the work, and if the class is new to group work, he may have to give fairly detailed guidance as to how the groups might set about their tasks. With experience, pupils will be able to plan their own methods reliably and confidently. Success in this may lead them to want to draw up their own specifications, and ultimately to take a greater part in the initial planning. The group-work teacher thus allows his children increasing responsibility, compatible with their own increasing self-confidence and with their proven abilities.

In the following excerpt the children show clearly that they fully appreciate—and relish—the role of the teacher (in this case, the students). These children had been writing and acting their own plays.

'What would you like to do from this point? Supposing the students were staying on—how would you see the thing going? Do you think they should stand back and let you get on with it?'

'Yes—no, we might get carried away and all act silly sometimes.'

'No, because we need some help, and some points we can't do properly, and they help us and then we can do them.'

'It's much better with the students than without. We're doing a comedy now, and we've got to a certain stage, and we kind of can't fit the rest in; we've got the end, but we can't get the middle.'

'You mean, you feel you know what *you* want to do, and what you want *them* to do is just to help you when you ask them. Is that it?'

'Yes.'

'Or do you want them to say: "Now we will do this", "Now we will do that", "Now we will do the other"?'

'Oh, no. Just to help us, and when we're doing a play, if we do something wrong, they usually tell us when we've done it, at the end. We ask people for comments on what we've done. They usually suggest things; you know, if we haven't done it quite right, they suggest other things we could do instead, and if we like them, you know, we do them ourselves.'

These children had a good deal of freedom within the framework of the subject that was being studied, but the overall direction had been given to them by the students. One criticism that is sometimes made of group work is that while the pupils may be interested enough in what they are doing, and their investigations may lead them to deal with important parts of the syllabus, there may also be whole areas which are not touched upon at all. The tutor asked the children who had been studying the production of power about this.

'What about the possibility of having missed things out? To what extent is this a problem—the missing out of important things?'

'Well, there are things you don't know but come across them when you think about them, and eventually you see this, and think about things and come across questions.'

'Do you feel there is any danger in this kind of work of leaving things out, or do you feel that your interest carries you over the ground to such an extent that you perhaps know more than you think?'

'Everybody wants to know more, don't they? Scientists want to know more.'

'And you found that you wanted to know more, or your companions wanted to know more, so you went on and on and on?'

'Well, we found out from books and paper cuttings.'

'You feel there aren't any gaps? Does anybody feel there might be gaps?'

'There's gaps in everything.'

'Everybody wants to know more'—this innocent and splendid assumption is the basic premiss of group work. The whole super-structure of constraint in a traditional teacher-directed lesson— the assumed need for the teacher's constant supervision, the system of rewards and punishments, the reliance on competition, on exhortation and on praise or reproof—stems from the assumption that the child will not learn unless he is obliged to in some way, by force, cajolery, trickery or fear. In group work, however, the assumption is exactly the opposite: given the opportunity, 'everybody wants to know more'.

One of the advantages claimed for group work is that it not only allows children to use their initiative in planning and carrying through their own investigations, but also provides opportunities for self-expression and the development of self-confidence. Here are some members of the group who wrote and acted their own plays, talking with the tutor about what they did.

'What have you been doing in your group?'
'Well, in our own group we are doing plays, and we have to rehearse it; first of all we do it without speech and after that we do it with the speech. This week we've dressed up for it.'
'Dressed up?'
'Yes.'
'And what sort of play are you doing?'
'This week it's a comedy.'
'And last week?'
'It was just straight acting last week.'
'Does this mean that each week you've done something different?'
'Yes.'
'What about your group?'
'We're doing comedy also, and it's called *The Light-Fingered Club and Cop Carey and the Cat Burglars*.'
'And did you make this up or did somebody else make it up?'
'We made it up.'
'And is this something that you're all doing, making up your plays, or are you in fact using plays that somebody has already written?'
'No, we make them up ourselves.'
'And how did you set about making them up? How do you decide that one is going to be a tragedy and one a comedy?'

'Well, we started off one with a plane crash, and we just thought it up as we were doing a project about planes. Then a couple of us were making jokes, and so we decided on a plane comedy.'

'So this tied up with something you were doing before?'

'Yes.'

'Have you done much of this before the students came here?'

'No, none.'

'Do you think this has been of any value to you? Have you gained anything from it?'

'Yes. Well, some of us are shy about speaking out in public, but now we aren't so shy, because of acting and that, and performing in front of the class.'

'We're used to people laughing at us and things like that. Some people want to take it up as a career. I think we ought to start with one bit of the play and build up to making up, acting and everything, and build it up into a really good play, perform it, and then show it again, and then talk all round about it.'

'I think I've learnt quite a lot from it—public speaking, acting, and all that, and quite a lot of other things.'

Certainly the member of the class who wanted to start with one bit of the play and build it up into a really good play was clearly demonstrating that 'everybody wants to know more'.

Another question the tutor was interested in was the extent to which the range of abilities of children within the group affected the work. Is it the case that the abler children were held back by their slower companions, or were the slow children left out of things? One of the children questioned about this answered in the following way:

'In a group you learn by your mistakes. You make a mistake and there's always someone who knows you've done wrong. And in a group when you're doing work, you can go on by yourself when there's a certain subject you're doing, and the rest of the group doesn't hold you back. But when you're in a big class, when you know something and the others don't, the teacher's got to keep going back to it. So if we're in a group, we can just go ahead.'

'How would you like groups made up? Would you like to be a member of a group with other children, some of whom are better than you, some of whom are not so good at their work? Or would you rather be in a group where you are all about the same?'

'I think if they are all different standards, because the ones that are cleverer would have a tendency to juggle the others up to their standards, you know.'

Nevertheless, it was recognized by the children that one of the problems of group work is the relationship of the members within the group. As one girl put it:

'I think you do need one person who is a bit better to be the leader. I mean, you can't all be saying: "We'll do this", "We'll do that", you need one person. But if an intelligent person leads the group, he'll get fed up with it, because all he'll have to do is just sit around telling them what to do. He'll want to do what he wants to do, won't he?'

Group work, then, has its problems. But they do not arise from the traditional bogies of the class teacher: reluctance to work, lack of interest, apathy and inattentiveness. Instead, they are problems of organization caused, for the most part, by the enthusiasm of the children in what they are doing, and by the need to ensure that they all have a chance to participate. For if it is true that 'everybody wants to know more', then it is necessary to provide the opportunity for everybody to find out more, and it is with the provision of this opportunity that group work is concerned.

The aim of this book is to make some suggestions as to how best to organize group work so as to anticipate these problems. These suggestions are based, not only upon the authors' own experience in teaching children and students, but also upon the experience of the students themselves, and upon that of the teachers under whom they have worked. In making them we should like to emphasize—and we are sure that we should be supported in this by both teachers and students concerned—that they are suggestions only. We are certainly not wishing to set up as authorities in the subject, and if we appear to be expressing ourselves dogmatically from time to time, it must be attributed to enthusiasm rather than to expertise. We both start from the conviction that such personal qualities as tolerance, generosity of spirit, friendliness, and a sympathetic understanding of children, coupled with an enthusiasm for learning and an avid curiosity, are far more important ingredients to good teaching than any particular method. In our capacity as supervisors, we have seen exciting and successful lessons that broke every rule in the textbooks, just as we have seen deadly dull lessons that have been based on a perfectly sound approach. Teaching is essentially a personal art, and every teacher has his or her own style. So we would emphasize that what follows are suggestions only, for the consideration of teachers and tutors, and not a fool-proof system for universal adoption by all teachers.

There is a further point. Group work is only one method of teaching. There are many others, including the traditional teacher-directed methods that have stood the test of time. We are not wishing to suggest that group work should be adopted as the one and only method, to the exclusion of all others. Team teaching, individual assignments, films and lectures, seminars and discussions, as well as formal lessons—they should, in our opinion, all have a place in the school of today, and we would ourselves regard the unthinking adoption of any one method, whether group work or not, as an approach foredoomed to failure.

Our concern in this book is not only with the problems of group-work methods themselves, but also with the problems of training students in these methods. We have therefore started with an account of a large-scale experiment in Bristol, in which a hundred students were placed in secondary schools for a morning a week during two terms, to try out group-work methods under the joint supervision of experienced members of the school staffs and college tutors. It is obvious that without the willing co-operation of the schools concerned, this experiment could not have been attempted, and we should like to emphasize the importance we ourselves attach to the fact that the whole venture was planned and carried out as co-operative enterprise. Too often colleges of education are thought of as unrealistic hothouses in which lecturers, themselves either not having taught a class of children for twenty years, or even totally without teaching experience, try to force fanciful methods based on high-falutin theories on credulous students. An alternative view is that colleges of education are hopelessly traditional and out of date, while all the progressive experiments in new methods of teaching are to be found in schools. Here, at any rate, was one development that was based on a joint venture by college and schools, with each appreciative of the contribution the other had to offer.

2

An experiment in the training of teachers

Students preparing to teach in secondary schools are traditionally given a training in teaching one or more subjects, and their course includes the academic study of the subjects themselves as well as professional training in how to teach them. In a college of education these two aspects proceed side by side; in a university the subjects are taken to degree level, and a fourth year is then devoted wholly to professional training (which includes, of course, the study of child psychology, educational sociology, and the aims and philosophy of education as well as the theoretical and practical study of methods of teaching). Traditionally, the course for intending secondary teachers—whether at college or university—is almost wholly subject-orientated. That is, it assumes that the teacher's main task will be the teaching of *subjects*: mathematics, history, physical education, and the like—in schools in which the day is divided into forty-minute periods and the children into thirty-pupil classes.

The students themselves normally come from grammar or public schools in which there is rarely any alternative to the subject timetable, and they themselves certainly expect to teach in the same way. Many of them are deeply interested in their subjects, and usually cite this interest as their reason for choosing to train for secondary teaching. Often they are led to choose teaching as a career as a direct result of the enthusiasm for his subject of one of their own teachers.

Inextricably interwoven with the tradition of subject teaching is the concept of the teacher as an authority in his subject, and from this concept flows the whole rationale of secondary-school 'method'. The theoretical problem is that of most efficiently organizing the communication of a body of knowledge from the one possessing it, the teacher, to the many seeking to possess it, the pupils. The traditional solution to this problem—the Herbartian steps of preparation, presentation, association, generalization and application—is still reflected in the arrangement of lesson notes many student teachers are required to prepare for their teaching practices.

This approach to teaching is still perfectly valid provided that two assumptions are justified: firstly, that there is *in fact* a recognized body of knowledge; and secondly, that the pupils do *in fact* seek to possess it. Given that these assumptions are correct, subject teaching can be successful and rewarding, and indeed most of those concerned with the training of secondary teachers consider that the development of appropriate methods of such teaching—though not necessarily along the lines suggested by Herbart and his followers—remain an important part of the professional training course.

However, it must be admitted that there are few teachers who can rely on both these assumptions being fully justified all the time. Most teachers have to deal, at some time or other, with pupils who are not 'positively motivated' towards learning what they are trying to teach, and for some teachers the majority of their children are uninterested in, bored with or even actively hostile towards the subject-matter they are being taught for much of the time. Such a situation leads, of course, to the traditional system of rewards and punishments, necessary only because the learning of the subject is not sufficient incentive in itself.

We are coming to realize, however, that the problems of teaching children who, for some reason, are uninterested in the subject is not the most important reason for querying the tradition of subject teaching. If this were so, this book would need to be addressed only to teachers of 'problem' children. A more far-reaching objection is the fact that the assumption that there exist relevant bodies of knowledge in the traditional subject areas which constitute appropriate curricula for secondary schools is being questioned. Or, to put the matter another way, the view is now rapidly gaining ground that the traditional secondary-school curriculum does not constitute the best preparation for further education in a fast-changing and technologically-orientated society. What is looked for in secondary school-leavers is not so much the possession of a large number of facts, but knowledge of, and ability to manipulate a much smaller stock of fundamental information, together with evidence of personal skills in investigation, interpretation and creative thinking. Such skills are not easily developed under a traditional subject-teaching approach.

THE SOURCES OF A CHANGE IN ATTITUDE TOWARDS SUBJECT TEACHING

The suggestion that something like the group-project approach of an enlightened primary school might be appropriate for secondary schoolchildren is not new. Group work, individual assignments, topic work—these have for a long time been regarded as alternatives to class lessons by progressive secondary teachers. What is perhaps new is the growing recognition on the part of the general body of the profession that these approaches, together with such activities as exhibitions, dramatic performances, excursions, work parties and the like, should form a normal and proper part of the secondary-school curriculum, and that the necessary expertise required in organizing and supervising them should therefore form a normal part of the secondary teacher's repertoire.

This change of attitude can be attributed to a number of sources. No doubt it is due in part to the work and influence of progressive schools both inside and outside the state system, as well as to such individual teachers as Caldwell Cook, A. D. Rowe and more recently, R. F. Mackenzie.[1] The recommendations of the Newsom Report[2] (one of the few Government reports to be widely read as well as referred to) were based largely on the best work of those secondary modern schools who took advantage of the freedom from the restraints of examination syllabuses to devise courses geared to the real needs of non-academic child-

[1] Cook (1919), Rowe (1959), Mackenzie (1965).
[2] Education, Ministry of (1963).

ren, and the Mode III entry to the C.S.E. has made it possible
for these advances to be continued with examination classes. The
slow acceptance of the findings of Piaget and his followers must
be in part attributed to the sheer difficulty of the texts but once
generally accepted, as they are now coming to be, they must call
into question the greater part of the traditional approach to
secondary teaching. Even the abolition of Christmas-leaving
afforded teachers an opportunity to plan a more meaningful
fourth-year course instead of being faced with having to teach
a class reduced by a third at the end of each term, while the
prospect of the raising of the school-leaving age to sixteen has
forced even the most dilatory of teachers to reconsider their
methods, and the Schools Council's working paper on the subject
has been widely read and discussed.[1]

In addition there have been other forces at work. The increased
size of secondary schools, and the inclusion of the whole range of
abilities under one roof in the comprehensive system, have
brought many teachers for their first time face to face with the
problem of teaching a wide range of intellectual and special
abilities within the same school. An affluent society has made it
possible for children to remain at school in families where, a
generation ago, their earnings would have been essential to the
household budget. Such young people expect a curriculum more
nearly suited to their needs than the traditional grammar-school
course affords.

But it must not be supposed that the re-examination of traditional secondary-teaching methods is brought about only by the
fact that schools have somehow to cope with the continued
education of children who, hitherto, have left school at fifteen
to enter a manual occupation—the intellectually average and
below-average constituting half our population, and sometimes
referred to as 'Newsom children'. The concern is much wider
and more basic than that. As we have said above, the traditional
subject-teaching approach, which is of course the grammar-school
approach, is based upon the assumption that there exist well-

[1] Schools Council (1966)

defined areas of knowledge—identified with the traditional subjects—which can be taught as established facts. With the present
rate of technological change—and this affects pure science just
as much as applied science, albeit more indirectly—this is increasingly seen to be, if not a false assumption, at least a very
limiting one. Universities, technical colleges, laboratories and
industry itself complain that sixth-form leavers arrive with their
heads crammed with irrelevant and often out-of-date information which they are unable to manipulate except within the narrow limits of responses to specific questions. Far too many
children—and this includes many of those who achieve success
in external examinations—learn their subjects through a combination of irrelevant associations and sheer rote memory which
not only prevents them from applying their knowledge in unfamiliar situations but also forms an almost insuperable barrier
to their being able to approach new problems in fresh ways.
Thus, not only are their minds encumbered with matter which
may well be of little use to them once their A levels have been
achieved, but also the manner by which they have acquired it
may have given them an approach to learning itself which is
totally inapplicable in their new circumstances.

There are, no doubt, those children who are able to amass,
coherently and meaningfully, the avalanche of facts presented
to them during their secondary-school course, and who, having
dutifully rehearsed them during their examinations, are then
able to re-examine them from an entirely fresh point of view,
dispense with what is no longer valid, and incorporate the remainder into a new intellectual structure. But such children are
few—perhaps not more than 10 per cent of an average grammar-
school intake at most. Perhaps another 15 per cent compen-
sate for a relative lack of intellectual flexibility by drawing upon
an exceptional capacity for retention and recall of unrelated
brute fact. The remaining 75 per cent rely, to a greater or lesser
degree, upon what John Holt has called (in *How Children Fail*,
one of the most fundamentally provocative books on education
to be published this century[1]) 'strategies of learning'—that is,

[1] Holt (1964)

ways of arriving at the correct answers through gimmicks, shrewd guesses, calculated likelihoods, through such cues as the teacher's tone of voice or expression, and even through entirely random associations. Such an approach is strictly comparable with the way in which a tribal magician conducts his relationship with the supernatural. Through a mixture of shrewd and wild guessing, of the observation of incidental phenomena and sheer mumbo-jumbo, he makes his predictions—and then sits back in trepidation to see if they come true. It is small wonder that subjects 'done' in this way prove sadly unsusceptible to subsequent manipulation.

If a fair proportion of so-called academic children learn in this way—and any grammar-school teacher who cares to examine his pupils' command of their knowledge, not by the giving of traditional tests, but by asking them to demonstrate its application to the world outside the classroom, will be obliged to agree that at least some of them do so—then how much greater must be the mental confusion of non-academic children when presented with syllabuses and methods designed, more or less explicitly, on the grammar-school curriculum.

The weight of the argument for reconsidering the grammar-school tradition of secondary teaching, therefore, derives as much from an uneasiness with the assumption that school subjects are coherent and relevant bodies of knowledge, as it does from an uneasiness with the assumption that all secondary school-children are equally anxious to acquire them. And while one can no doubt discover many worthy and even some successful teachers who see no reason for changing matters, yet it would be fair to say that dissatisfaction with the traditional methods as well as with the traditional content of the secondary-school course as the sole approach to learning offered to today's teenagers is no longer confined to a few, but is becoming pretty general among teachers and educationists of all kinds.

IMPLICATIONS FOR THE TRAINING OF TEACHERS

These considerations put a responsibility upon those concerned with the preparation of secondary teachers to provide in their course of training experience of a variety of approaches which might prove alternatives to the traditional methods associated with subject teaching. As part of this experience it was decided at one college of education—following upon a successful pilot scheme the previous year with a small number of students—to give all those students preparing to teach in secondary schools an opportunity to take part in working with small groups of children on projects which cut across existing subject boundaries. It should perhaps be emphasized that this was not seen by the tutors, nor indeed presented to the students, as a substitute for class teaching, but as an alternative method which might be more appropriate in certain circumstances, and which should therefore form a normal part of the secondary teacher's repertoire.

Group work is not, of course, the only alternative to class teaching. Team teaching, class projects, individual assignments all offer approaches which break away from the traditional classroom situation. From the point of view of training teachers, however, group work affords a number of important advantages. Students are suspicious of any method with which they are unfamiliar and they are particularly unhappy if they suspect that they are being used as guinea pigs in order to try out some new approach. Group work has long been an accepted method in primary teaching and has a well-established rationale. While it is true that in group work with older children the teacher's role is somewhat different from that which the primary teacher adopts, the difference is largely one of degree, and the fact that students preparing to use group work in secondary schools knew that their class-mates were successfully applying this approach in primary schools gave them confidence that it definitely 'worked' as a teaching method. Secondly, by attaching students not to a whole class but to a small group of children, it was possible to give them an opportunity to learn for themselves and at first hand how a group, given the freedom to pursue their own lines of investigation, can develop an intellectual dynamic and, more important, an emotional commitment to their investigation which is quite different in quality from the attitude even of enthusiastic pupils in a class lesson. There was also the incidental advantage of giving students the chance to get to know well, and in a relatively informal situation, a small number of children. Thirdly, while group work need not necessarily be based on an inter-disciplinary approach, by acting on the suggestion that their schemes could be in areas other than the students' own main subjects, they were able to discover for themselves the impetus to learning which a departure from well-trodden paths can engender. And fourthly, by working initially with only a single group of children they were able to gain insight into group work as a viable method which could give them the necessary confidence to embark upon it with a whole class on a subsequent occasion.

A LARGE-SCALE TRAINING PROGRAMME

Having decided that some experience in group work was a desirable part of every secondary and junior-secondary student's education course, it became necessary to see how such a programme could be carried out. In so far as this was regarded as something which should be given in addition to experience of other methods, it was felt that it should not replace any of the existing teaching-practice periods but should somehow be provided in addition. This had obvious implications for the schools, many of them already over-used for normal teaching practice, and it was clearly essential to obtain the teachers' co-operation. But there was a more important reason than that of expediency why it was felt necessary to consult the teachers at the outset. The college was fortunate in having in its teaching-practice schools a fair number of secondary teachers either already experienced in group work, or enthusiastic about experimenting with it. It was seen that this circumstance gave the opportunity for a co-operative approach to the training of students in which teacher, tutor and student could work together in a functional relationship. Such an approach was appropriate in a programme which was itself experimental.

To this end, a meeting was held at the college of the heads and members of staff of schools with the tutors concerned, to work

GWSS—B

out jointly a training programme. A number of resolutions were adopted at the meeting, including the working principle that while group work might be particularly appropriate for C.S.E. classes and for work with 'Newsom children', it should not be regarded as a method of teaching suitable only for average and below-average children, but could be adapted for the teaching of appropriate parts of the syllabus for children of all ages and all levels of ability. In particular, it was suitable for work with mixed-ability classes.

The fact that so many experienced teachers in the local schools were already using a variety of informal teaching methods meant that students could benefit in this aspect of their training by working in co-operation with and under the guidance of those teachers in their own schools. There was, therefore, a minimum of artificiality in the situation, and an important incidental objective of the training programme was the co-operation between tutor and teacher, college and school, for the development of the student in work of this kind with secondary children.

A frequent and often valid criticism of teaching practice is that there exists a lack of integration between the work of schools and the work of students in training who are later to work in those schools. Genuinely shared responsibility for aspects of the training helps to reduce this failure and helps the student to become involved with the reality of the classroom situation in a more direct and positive way.

Because of the fund of experience among the teachers in group-work methods, it was decided that, as a preliminary to the students themselves being responsible for the children's work, they should in the first instance work alongside the teachers in their classes with the children, helping with the teachers' own schemes. This would enable them to become familiar with the school itself and its organization and facilities, and to get to know the children, before having to cope with the organizational problems involved. During this stage of 'apprenticeship', the students would be free to observe as well as to participate, and to begin to plan in consultation with teachers and tutors in pre-paration for the next stage in the training programme when they would be responsible for the work of the children and the teachers' role would then become an advisory one.

For the first stage of the programme the teachers outlined the various schemes that were in progress in the schools and the students were invited to form themselves into groups of between two and five members in order to select from the topics offered. They were encouraged, in forming these groups, to combine different subjects and interests. Thanks to the wide variety of schemes offered by the teachers and thanks also to the imaginative approach of the students themselves it was found possible to allocate nearly all of over a hundred students to topics of their first choice to work for a morning a week under the guidance of the teachers for the second half of a term.

In this way the students found themselves not only working on schemes that were already different from those of a normal subject approach, but also working with other students with different subject interests from their own. Students with commerce as their main subject found that handicraft, history or drama students approached the topics that were their common concern from a different but equally valid viewpoint.

While each student was attached to a small group of 6-8 children, they were expected to plan together a scheme of their own for the next term's work. They would continue to work with the same groups of children, but would accept joint responsibility for the work as a whole, under the supervision of teacher and visiting college tutors.

In the event, the schemes of work varied considerably. Some students carried on with an elaboration of the schemes that the teachers had initiated. Others planned entirely new programmes with the whole class working on a common theme, of which each group took a different aspect and reported back to the rest from time to time. In one or two groups each of the students pursued a separate topic with his or her own pupils. To be fair to the students, the teachers themselves had different expectations about what they should do: some gave the students complete freedom of planning while others expected them to carry on where they themselves left off. What was common to all groups was the investigation of some topic or the pursuit of some activity in which the pupils themselves took an active part and worked in small groups, each under the guidance of a student. Some examples of topics were:

The production of a play based on a clash between coloured and white youths in a coffee bar.

A general survey of three postal districts based on visits, leading to a community services map.

A project on the production of power with groups working on coal, the grid system, the North Sea project, the use of electricity, and including visits to power stations and sub-stations.

A project on law and order, approached historically by groups choosing different periods, and by a study of law and order today.

The history of the written word: picture-writing, stories, the history of paper.

A study of timber, involving practical work in the forest, and a study of its production.

A study of road maps, lorry routes, holiday routes, etc., leading to scale drawings and co-ordinate geometry.

The construction of a mobile from polystyrene to decorate the library.

A study of a local river, including a week's canoeing and camping expedition.

House management and budgeting.

The production of a marionette theatre.

A survey of newspaper reading.

The building of an engineering workshop.

A study of the telephone, including its history, telephone engineering, telephone exchanges, radio and television.

Trees in the neighbourhood.

One problem that concerned the tutors involved was the extent to which the students should be taught how to do group work. They were second-year students, and had therefore already spent two continuous periods in schools, one largely for observation, the other for teaching-practice purposes, as well as having visited a number of schools for observation and other work. The empha-

sis during the first year, as far as their professional training
had been concerned, was mainly on traditional methods of teaching. For those students preparing to teach only in secondary
schools, this was equated for the most part with class lessons,
though of course the emphasis had been placed on pupil participation and learning through discovery and experience, but within
the framework of a formal approach. Education and supervising
tutors had stressed that, even within a formal framework, there
was no *one* best way to teach, and that each student had to discover a personal style, in which some of the various suggestions
made during the course would prove appropriate while others
would not. It was felt that to attempt to specify a particular
technique of group work would be to depart from this general
principle. Moreover, the tutors were anxious to prevent the
students themselves from trying to force the children in their
turn into following a predetermined approach.

For this reason, apart from discussing the general principles
involved, there were no specific preparatory classes arranged
in college. Tutorials and discussions were held with individuals
and groups of students to deal with specific points as they arose,
and occasional talks were given from time to time, during the
progress of the second stage of the group work, on aspects of
organization, the psychology of small groups, display, and feedback in group work, attendance at which was voluntary. One of
the most valuable meetings was held halfway through the second
term when a panel of tutors and students combined in college to
hold an open forum. It was probably this session more than
any other which persuaded the majority of students that there is
no one special technique in group work. Here there was a free
exchange of widely divergent views both between and among
the students and tutors concerned, with evidence of insight and
successful achievement arising from a variety of different experiences.

The value of training is not restricted to the learning of expertise. The students were required to assess their activities and to
record their progress, noting failures as well as successes. To
this end each group of students maintained a log book which also

included the plans of each week's work together with any alterations made during the day. It was interesting to see from these records how the standard of values changed as the work progressed and as the students themselves came to know the children individually. Two mature students, who had given up jobs in industry to train as teachers, began their entries with concern about the intellectual capacity of the children they were working with in relation to what they hoped to do, only to wax poetical some weeks later about the fact that a child, notorious in the school for his former lack of co-operation and aggressiveness, not only had successfully mapped and recorded the telephone kiosks of the district, as part of a project on telephones, but also had grasped unaided the fact that an oscilloscope transmits sound waves in light form. A group of girls regarded with grave suspicion at first as potential delinquents and trouble-makers by some other students were found to be friendly and helpful—so public-spirited in fact that they regularly attended a children's day nursery to give practical help in the care of small children. Another group, loosely described as 'non-academic' leavers, wrote and recorded a sensitive play based on colour prejudice among young people their own age.

In this way the students discovered unexpected potentialities in the children, and by helping the children to realize them, revealed latent capacities of their own.

Another general feature that emerged with many students in their evaluations was that as a result of their contact with teachers in a freer situation, the children were able to present the more positive side of themselves, an aspect which can easily become submerged in the demand for conformity in a class teaching situation. As a result the students more easily understood the children's reactions to difficulties, and working on a more intimate level, were able to help them to overcome them.

It was not only the students who were asked to evaluate their experiences. Before the programme ended, an evaluative conference was held at the college in which working parties of tutors and teachers who had participated discussed the whole training scheme under a number of headings, to make recommendations for the future and to report to a plenary session so that full discussion would take place on the recommendations from each working party.[1]

The value of the programme was rated highly by all those taking part, not least because it led to a degree of involvement in training between the schools and the college which might not otherwise have been attained. The teachers were more directly concerned, in planning as well as in supervision, than is often usual in a normal teaching practice. The children were participating in an altogether freer situation than occurs in a formal class lesson, and because of this, and because of the small groups, the students came to know them as individuals, each with his or her own contribution to make to the work as a whole. This in turn led to a response on the part of the students that was quite different from the 'them and me' attitude of normal teaching practice.

[1] A report from this conference is given below in an appendix, page 123.

3 *The nature of group work*

The experiment described in the last chapter proceeded from a conviction on the part of college education tutors that students preparing to teach in secondary schools should, as part of their training in classroom methods, be given experience in group work in addition to the more usual teacher-directed methods normally adopted on their teaching practices. As we have said, it was felt to be inconsistent with the idea of a personal style of teaching that 'the best way of doing group work' should be taught (even supposing that the tutors had been able to agree as to what it was!); on the other hand it was clearly unreasonable to expect students to deal with a method of which most of them had no personal experience, without some guidance. A compromise which was adopted was to suggest certain essential principles, departures from the spirit of which would—in the view of the tutors—seriously detract from the value and success of the group-work approach, and to outline various organizational procedures which would be in keeping with these essentials. The aim of the present chapter is to discuss these principles, very much in the way that they were discussed with the students.

DISTINCTION BETWEEN GROUP WORK AND GROUP TEACHING

In order to examine the essential principles of group work it is necessary at the outset to make a distinction between the kind of group work we are speaking of here, and what is sometimes referred to as 'formal group work', or what we will call *group teaching*. This latter is a method sometimes used by teachers to deal with a wide range of abilities within a single class. With group teaching the children are divided by the teacher into several groups on the basis of their academic attainment in the subject being taught, and each group is then dealt with by the teacher separately. While he is explaining something to one group, the remainder of the class may be getting on with some written work. Alternatively, all groups may be doing written work (differing from group to group according to the range of abilities), while the teacher goes round the class giving his attention to individual pupils.

With group teaching the division of children into groups may be a more or less permanent affair with little change in the membership of the groups from week to week, or it may be a very flexible arrangement with the teacher forming and reforming groups during a single lesson.

Group teaching calls for careful preparation and a good deal of mental agility on the teacher's part. It differs from the kind of group work we are concerned with here in a number of important ways. One is that the criterion for the formation of groups in group teaching is that of academic aptitude. Indeed, it is no more than the logical extension of the system of academic streaming by which most large schools divide their children into classes in the first place.[1]

Now the division of children into groups on the basis of their academic aptitude may well seem a perfectly sensible procedure if we accept the assumption that there is a fundamental division of labour intrinsic to the classroom situation: the division between the role of the teacher, whose job it is to teach, and the role of the children, whose job it is to learn. In such a situation, the teacher's task is seen as an active one; he is responsible for the preparation and planning of the lesson, and for its direction and administration. The children's role is largely passive. Their task is to do what the teacher tells them to do. This is not to say, of course, that the children are necessarily still and quiet. 'Learning by doing' is a favourite catchword of twentieth-century

[1] In Britain and South Africa, though not to the same extent in most countries of the world; see Jackson (1964) pp. 127-9 and, for a detailed analysis of the situation, Yates (1966).

education and every college tutor will stress the importance of the pupils' participation in a successful lesson. But this activity on the part of the pupils is seen as essentially teacher-directed. After all, the teacher is usually the only person present in the classroom who knows where the class is heading; he has access to the syllabus (which in any case he may have drawn up himself), and he is also the fount of knowledge. In such circumstances it may be sensible enough to divide children into ability groups or streams within a class, so that the teacher can deal most efficiently with each group.[1]

We may call this view of the two roles of teacher and child, and this approach to the teacher's task, *directed* teaching. We need not even say 'teacher-directed', since if there is to be direction, it is taken for granted that it must come from the teacher himself. In directed teaching—that is to say in the teaching that goes on in a large majority of the classrooms of the secondary schools of Britain—the responsibility for the selection of subject-matter, the manner in which it is treated, the presentation and development of the topic, the nature and extent of oral and written work by the pupils, the selection and use of textbooks and audio-visual aids, the questions set in the lesson and for homework, the extent and manner in which the topic is followed up—the responsibility for all these is the teacher's, as indeed it is for the arrangement of the furniture, the selection of charts and other matter displayed on the notice-boards, and even the questions of whether or not the windows should be open or the lights on.

A second and more important way in which group work differs from group teaching is that in the latter the children are divided into groups by the teacher, whereas in group work the children themselves choose which group they wish to join on the basis of its proposed activities.

The adoption of the children's own free choice as the criterion

[1] Though it should be pointed out that two of the basic assumptions of such streaming, whether within the class or within the school as a whole—that the academic aptitudes of children are (i) innate, and (ii) able to be measured accurately—would no longer be accepted without question by the majority of educational psychologists today.

of division into groups is an essential principle of group work. This is not to say that the teacher plays no part in the process. It may be that he sometimes has to help a pupil make his choice. He can do this by outlining the proposed activities of the different groups beforehand, or he may remind the pupil of those of his own skills and declared interests which appear to be relevant to them. In either case, he is seeking to make the choice more meaningful to the pupils. What he must not do is to make the choice *for* the pupil. It is an important condition of group work, as described in this book, that each member of a group is a member by choice.

In choosing which group to join then, the child has regard to the proposed activity of the group and to his own interests and abilities (including, of course, his academic ability). There is a further consideration which may influence his choice, and that is who are the other members of the group. For many children, whom they are going to work with is as important as what they are going to work at. This is a second area in which the teacher should avoid trying to influence the child. It is as necessary for the success of the group that its members should, as far as possible, choose each other, as that they should choose what they are going to do. However, while the teacher should not prevent a child from joining a group of his choice, he should not allow the group itself to prevent other children from joining it.

Thus, in contradistinction to the group-teaching group, which is teacher-selected, the group-work group is self-selected.

The third vital difference between group teaching and group work is that in the former the activities of the group are directed by the teacher, while in group work the activities of the group are directed by the group itself. Now this does not mean that the group has total autonomy in running its own affairs. In the first place, its work—that is to say, the task for which it was formed— is normally decided on beforehand. In the second place, the teacher may expect to be called upon to give guidance and advice to its members on carrying out this work. And in the third place, there may be occasions on which the teacher deems it proper to take a part in the work of the group without waiting to be

invited, though it may be said here that the extent to which he
feels it necessary to take over its direction is a measure of the
failure of the approach itself. Ultimately, of course, the teacher
is responsible for the class and it is possible that an activity
embarked on by a group constitutes a genuine danger to the
children's safety, or threatens to damage valuable equipment.
Even in such cases, the teacher should content himself in the
first place with pointing out the danger or threat, and should
interfere only if the precautions taken as a result seem to him
inadequate.

A WORKING DEFINITION OF GROUP WORK

In the main, however, the members of the group decide upon
the plan of action in carrying out the work and they are then
responsible for putting the plan into effect. This leads to a
further characteristic of group work: the group constitutes its
own critic and judge of the work in progress. When activities are
teacher-directed, the children submit their work to the teacher
for judgement. In addition, the teacher may be expected to criti-
cize work in progress. The pupil's part in this is again passive;
he waits to be told what is right and what is wrong with his efforts.
It is true that teachers may try to develop in their pupils the
faculty of self-criticism, but they rarely allow such self-criticism,
even when it is manifest, to go unchecked by themselves. With
group work, however, it is quite usual for considerable parts of
the work to go unchecked, and even unseen, by the teacher.
Moreover, when the teacher does check progress and notices
some omission or error, he should avoid pointing out what is
wrong, but instead should ask questions, thereby leading the
group to realize its own mistake. In this way the teacher
underlines that the responsibility for checking is the group's
own.

From this we can arrive at a working definition of group
work as a method of teaching in which activities or tasks are
carried out by small groups of pupils, such groups being self-
selected and self-directed.

THE TEACHER'S ROLE

From what has been said so far it will be clear that the success of group work depends to a very large extent upon the attitude of the teacher and upon the manner in which he fulfils his own role with regard to it. Much of its educational value will be lost if the teacher, having specified the work carefully, and having allowed the groups to be formed with due regard to the children's free choice, then proceeds to play too direct a part in the carrying out of the work itself. Throughout the work, the aim of the teacher should be to stimulate the children to accept responsibility themselves for its progress, and to form their own judgements as to whether or not it is satisfactory. He can do this best by refusing to act as judge and critic himself on the occasions—and at first there will be many of them—when he is appealed to. Thus, when a tentative plan of action has been drawn up by the group and he is asked for his opinion on whether or not it will be successful, he should throw the question back at the group by asking them in turn why they think it should not be. He should get them to explain to him what circumstances they have made provision for, and what not. If there are faults in the plan apparent to his own eyes, he should try to get the members of the group to discover these for themselves, rather than draw their attention to them directly. All the time he should be working towards the situation in which the children come to rely less and less upon his advice, and more and more upon their own initiative and judgement.

The teacher's scope is wide. It is not his job to direct, but rather to follow and from time to time support and advise. But his advice is by no means mandatory and may be accepted or rejected either in part or in toto. For this reason any attempt on his part to ensure a particular end product would be a falsification and would frustrate the main point about working in this way. If he thinks something should be done at a certain stage he must show why. If he is unconvincing, his advice should not be taken. Ideally, his role is that of promoter and co-planner at the outset, but thereafter he should allow himself to be used more as a sounding-board than as a source of new information or new ideas. His extra knowledge and experience can better be used in helping the inquirer to ask the appropriate question than in answering questions the child has not yet formulated, or giving information the child is capable of finding for himself.

This is not to say that the teacher should always wait for his pupils to appeal to him before he draws their attention to mistakes they may be making, though he should always allow sufficient time for children to realize their own mistakes before he takes any action. Supposing it to be evident that no member of the group has spotted an error however, and supposing that the group is about to embark on the scheme which the teacher sees is foredoomed to failure—what should he then do? This is one of those situations in which he has to decide whether the lesson to be learnt from the failure of the enterprise is more valuable than the enterprise itself. Against this, he must set the effects of failure upon the members of the group; whether or not it will act as a spur to better action next time, or whether it might not discourage the diffident altogether. Another consideration is that of the cost of the materials; it may be that expensive materials or apparatus are involved, and that therefore mistakes cannot be afforded. It may be said, though, that this is hardly a favourable circumstance in which to learn self-reliance, and we would argue in favour of undertaking for group work only those activities in which a certain amount of wasted materials can be tolerated. The issue is not always clear-cut, however; it may be that the teacher has agreed that the class should contribute towards making some important addition to the school generally: the making of a tool shed, for instance, or the redecoration of a room. The effect on the children's own self-esteem in doing something of palpable value must be set against the limitations arising from the expense of the materials.

Thus the first question the teacher must always ask himself before pointing out any errors in plans of work is whether or not the child in question will benefit more from making the mistake than from correcting it beforehand, and this is true whether the mistake is a small one, affecting only one child and a tiny part of the total plan, or a major one, affecting the whole group, and the success or failure of the plan itself.

Should he decide that it would be better if the mistake were corrected, the teacher should then seek a way by which he can get the child to see his error for himself, and particularly a way by which the likelihood of his making the same or similar errors next time is lessened. Simply to point out the mistake is only to ensure that this particular mistake is corrected. To ask specific questions, the answers to which lead the child to discover the mistake, is an improvement. But best of all is the asking of general questions in such a way that not only is their application to this situation sufficient to discover the error, but also their application to all similar situations is liable to reveal similar errors. In this way the pupil can anticipate the teacher's help next time by asking those general questions himself. Thus the teacher again leads the child to accept responsibility for his own work.

To refrain from pointing out mistakes, to allow children to learn from their errors, to try to get them to see their mistakes for themselves—these precepts usually prove to be the most difficult of all for the inexperienced group-work teacher to act upon, since they seem to be in direct opposition to many generally-accepted principles of good teaching. We are told—for example by the manufacturers of teaching machines—that correct actions need to be reinforced and errors pointed out as soon as possible after they have been made. And it is often stated that the performance of wrong actions, without their immediate correction, makes the future repetition of them more likely by the simple effect of the so-called law of exercise. Part of what we are here arguing for is not, in fact, in opposition to these principles. By getting the pupil himself to examine his plan of action for possible errors, we are trying to arrive at the situation where he corrects his mistakes *before* he makes them. This is an obvious improvement on correcting them afterwards, no matter how soon. Moreover, the group-work approach is concerned with engendering (and be it noted, *engendering* and not conditioning) a critical and reasoning attitude towards work, not a series of non-thinking, semi-automatic aversive responses. Part of the conscious acceptance of responsibility for one's own work is based upon the full awareness of this possibility of error; in the development of such acceptance a reasonable history of actual error is a necessary condition.

The teacher should also expect regular progress reports from the groups, and should, from time to time, ask individual pupils to give a reasoned account of what they are doing and why. For his own part, the teacher should submit progress reports to careful scrutiny, being ready to point out any discrepancies between plans and work actually carried out. Though again, children experienced in group work should have recorded reasons for any departures from plans, and should be prepared to argue them on a rational basis.

It has been said above that the inexperienced group-work teacher will find the deliberate avoidance of pointing out mistakes the most difficult part of his task. His next most difficult problem will be that of doing nothing! He will have to accustom himself to a passive role and to accept that, other things being equal, the less he is legitimately occupied in dealing with his pupils, the better his teaching is going. This indeed is a complete reversal of the normal teaching situation and one that the beginner will find particularly trying to his self-esteem. We are wont to think that so long as we are actively employed in the classroom, we must be usefully employed in it, and we are apt to put aside (impatiently or guiltily, according to our beliefs) questions of how far the children are actually learning what we are so busy teaching. And in any case, what with preparing our lessons thoroughly, getting teaching aids together, making charts and taking photographs to enliven our lessons, ordering samples, planning visits, setting and marking written work, we simply have no time to consider such questions. The lesson depends upon us, the classroom centres round us and this, we feel, is how it should be. When we come to group work, we find we have suddenly become redundant—or so it seems. Once the children are embarked upon their several tasks—sometimes with a degree of purposefulness and enthusiasm that frankly surprises us—we find we have long stretches of time in which there appears to be nothing for us to do. We can even leave the classroom and return ten minutes later and nobody seems to have missed us. If we are entirely honest with ourselves, we are even jealous of the involvement which our pupils now have with their work, and if we are human, we miss their old dependence on ourselves. It takes some time before we are comfortable in our new role and for a long while we are apt to feel guilty because, although everything is going well, we are doing nothing ourselves.

Nevertheless, it is through an active participation on the part of the child that learning is acquired. Moreover, since each child needs a different starting-point, it must have the freedom to begin at that point and not at some other point pre-determined by the teacher. It is just this kind of freedom for learning that is provided by work of this kind. Futhermore, each child brings his own experience to bear in the acquisition of new learning skills and new information. What one child may already know, another may have yet to experience and learn. Where the regime is formal or over-directed by the teacher, all the children in a class are assumed by the teacher to start from the same point. Well may he wonder that some can 'follow' and others, although exposed to the same teaching, cannot understand. It is probably this factor more than any other that leads some educationalists to the view that group work is suitable only for the less-gifted child since, once the child really has the freedom to work at his own pace and level of investigation, he does just that and regresses to levels of working below that which the educator has conceived in his own wisdom to be appropriate. A child may accept and remember what he has read or copied out, he may reproduce from memory what he has been told at the fitting moment, but this does not mean to say that he comprehends what he knows. Consequently, when he is given the opportunity to take logical steps from that point into further areas of knowledge, he falters, is unable to do so and reverts to another level of working, one at which he does comprehend. This does not condemn the freedom of the method for working in group work, but the method of acquiring information up to that point. Hence the importance of the child's freedom to choose, and to become involved thereby, with the consequent diminishment of the teacher's own active participation.

Now it must not be supposed from this that the group-work teacher has a life of ease! Far from it. For it must be apparent by now that the success of a group-work undertaking depends to a very large extent upon the preparation beforehand; the extent to which the teacher has based his specifications upon his real understanding of his children's interests, enthusiasms and capacities; the extent to which he has allowed for a good deal of flexibility within them; the extent to which he has anticipated problems of their execution, and is ready with suggestions as to how these problems might be approached; the extent to which he has himself traced sources, ordered reference books for the library and classroom, laid in a good stock of materials likely to be needed, made preliminary approaches to various outside agencies which the children might want to contact (though without necessarily making known any of these prior activities to the children themselves); the extent to which he has worked out the procedure for discussions, working parties, group-formation, the keeping of records, voting, the allocation of tasks and so forth, so that the momentum of the work itself is never lost through any failure on his part to be ready with the requisite machinery for any given step; the extent, in other words, to which he has thought through, realistically and in detail, the whole of the work which he hopes will be accomplished. The success of any piece of group work—given that the essential principles of self-selection described above have been faithfully kept to—will depend to a large extent upon the teacher's concern with these details and it is, accordingly, to a consideration of them that we turn our attention in the next chapter.

4 *The organization of group work*

The aim of the present chapter is to put forward some organizational procedures which experience suggests enable the teacher to get the best out of a group-work approach. It must be emphasized, however, that these details, though important, are not of themselves sufficient to ensure success, and that adherence to the principles outlined in the previous chapter—of self-selected and self-directed groups—is an essential prior consideration. Given such adherence, then the following factors become of significance in planning group work, and teachers and students considering this approach for the first time would be well advised to give careful thought to them in their preparation.

THE TIME AVAILABLE

The organization of group work, particularly in its initial stages, and especially with children unused to it, takes up a fair amount of time. Normally, a double period on a conventional school timetable (that is, at least one hour and twenty minutes) is the minimum amount of time in which to begin group work unless both teacher and pupils have had a good deal of experience in it, in which case it is just possible (though usually extremely frustrating) to embark on an activity within a single period. Two hours is a better period of time for each session unless a visit is involved; a longer period may lead to weariness (though seldom to boredom).

Similarly, a certain minimum number of lessons is essential if the work is to be carried through satisfactorily, though this minimum will naturally vary according to the nature of the activity in question. However, we would venture a guess that an

absolute minimum number of lessons in which anything worthwhile could be undertaken might be four, assuming each lesson
is a double period. This gives eight standard timetable periods.
Most group-work activities will take at least twice that number,
and many will run on for longer, though there is a danger of
an activity losing its impetus through being dragged out, and
this is especially true with classes unused to group work. Teachers
preparing a project for children who are accustomed to a more
formal, directed approach are therefore advised to plan in such
a way that the work can be brought to a satisfying conclusion
within the compass of a single term's work. On the other hand,
once children become experienced in group work it will be found
that new areas for further work arise out of any given project,
and that consequently one activity leads naturally to others. With
such a situation, an experienced teacher may be able to plan with
confidence a whole year's work in such a way that he can see
how essential parts of his syllabus will be covered.

THE SPECIFICATION OF THE WORK: CONTENT

We may use the term *specification* to mean the definition of the
proposed outcome of the group work—whether it be a model,
a report, a display, a film, a play, a brochure, a map, or a
combination of these or other outcomes. This is probably the
most important single factor governing the success of group work
with inexperienced classes and it is therefore one to which the
teacher should give special attention and planning beforehand. A
successful group-work undertaking, particularly with children
unused to this approach, is nearly always one in which the group
had a very clear idea beforehand of what they were attempting
to achieve. And it is in determining the specification of the work
that the skill of the teacher is most tested, for he must be prepared
to allow the children as much initiative in this as is compatible
with their experience and interests, while at the same time having
regard to the needs of his syllabus and his knowledge of their
capabilities.

With classes new to group work the teacher might be wise to

draw up the specification beforehand in some detail, but he should be prepared, in discussing the project with the class, to modify his plans if the children make their own suggestions. Perhaps the most effective way of doing this is not to reveal at first the full details of the work, but to state the general intention and to invite suggestions from the class. If none are forthcoming, he can then fill in some details from his plan, always being ready to listen to comments and suggestions from the children, and to modify his own ideas when their proposals are practicable.

This is, in fact, much more difficult than it sounds. It is very easy for the enthusiastic teacher to become wedded to his own ideas to such an extent that he is unwilling to relinquish them for the ideas of the children. For one thing, his own ideas are probably much better. For another, he is likely to base his estimates of the children's capabilities upon what they have done in a teacher-directed situation, whereas if they are allowed some measure of initiative, children often reveal entirely unsuspected talents and enterprise. The principle by which the teacher should be guided, and of which he may have constantly to remind himself, is that the quality, originality and general attractiveness of the outcome of the work is far less important than the extent to which it is a genuine reflection of the children's own enterprise and effort.

This is not to say that the teacher should not concern himself with standards. Of course he will want the end-product to be as carefully presented, as accurate, as lively and as attractive as the children can make it. But these desiderata should be achieved not through the teacher's direct intervention, nor through his insistence upon them, but as a result of the children's own developing critical standards. A high critical standard in judging one's own work is something that many adults find it difficult to achieve. The teacher must therefore be patient and not expect its achievement in his pupils at a single bound. What he can be sure of is that if he takes it upon himself to act as uninvited critic he is likely to delay, if not to prevent altogether, the development of self-criticism in his class.

There is a further important proviso. Even where a teacher

deems it necessary to draw up a detailed specification, he should —as far as possible—limit the details to the proposed outcome, and avoid prescribing exactly the methods by which that outcome is to be achieved. It is in deciding upon the appropriate method, and in evaluating its success, that the initiative of the children can be best exercised. The extent to which the teacher decides upon the methods—to that extent he is depriving his pupils of the main value of the group-work approach. This does not mean, of course, that he will have no say in the method. He is certain to be consulted by the group as to the wisdom of this or that plan of action. And here again, unless he can see that the suggested plan is likely to lead to frustration without any incidental benefits, he should try to content himself with asking questions, rather than with passing judgement on the proposals. (Apart from anything else, he might be wrong in his predictions!) His concern must always be to try to get the group to think for themselves, and to accept responsibility for their own decisions. At the same time, he should not allow them to experience unnecessary frustration on account of their unawareness of the mistakes they are making, or because they do not know what to do next.

The teacher's role is thus a difficult and subtle one. He must try, through judicial questioning, to get the group to find their own solutions, while at the same time being prepared to come in with advice where they are genuinely stumped. And he should always be ready with praise and encouragement, even where mistakes have been made, so that his pupils come to see that the mistakes themselves are a source of further learning and discovery.

It should perhaps be emphasized that the above suggestions regarding the detailed drawing up of specifications refer only to classes inexperienced in group work. With greater experience and confidence, the children themselves will take on the responsibility of defining the specification, though even here the generalization still holds good that a successful outcome nearly always depends upon a clear idea beforehand of what the group is aiming at. This does not mean, of course, that plans may not be very considerably modified during the course of the work, nor that short-term aims may not well develop into further long-term aims.

THE SPECIFICATION OF THE WORK: SOURCES

There are three main sources from which group work may be derived: the syllabus, the teacher's interests, the pupils' interests. It is not essential for the success of group work that it derives entirely from children's interests, though it is true that many successful activities do so. What *is* necessary is that the pupils are given free rein to their initiative in realizing the aim of the work—that is the essential ingredient. Teachers who wish to keep closely to their syllabuses may therefore decide to select a particular topic for group work. It is important that the topic should lend itself to some kind of joint activity by a group: the solving of simple problems in area does not, for example, whereas the estimation of the cost of decorating a room may do so (though it is a somewhat limited exercise in itself unless it is a preliminary to the decoration itself). The closer the work can be linked to some real and desired outcome, the more successful it is likely to be. Thus, the preparation of a plan of an imaginary building is of limited value; a plan of a real building is of greater value; a plan of a school building for which alterations are being considered is better still; and if that plan is in fact going to be used by the Headmaster in discussing the alterations with governors and local authorities, then an ideal situation has been found. The production of maps and plans, the carrying out of surveys, the design and testing of equipment and apparatus, the planning and carrying out of masques, concerts, operas, festivals and pageants, and of school entertainments and exhibitions, the making of films, dramatic performances, the investigation of problems concerning school administration and maintenance, taking part in social services, the organization of appeals, the production of newspapers and magazines, the decoration and repair of premises, the planning and carrying out of excursions and holidays— these are all suitable activities which lend themselves to group work.

The teacher may wish to follow his own particular interests in suggesting a topic for group work. And it may be appropriate that he should, especially if the class is in a transitional stage between directed teaching and group methods of working. Even so, this does not imply that he should dictate the detail, content or method of working, and even where a topic has been promoted by the teacher, the formation of the groups, working framework and internal group organization can be arranged by the children. If he does suggest his own topic, he should take care that his own enthusiasm does not blind him to the limitations of what he proposes. There is a further possible drawback to following the teacher's interests and that is that the temptation to interfere with the activities of the group is that much greater, especially if they involve methods with which the teacher himself is very familiar. This problem is heightened by the fact that he may well apply standards to the children's work that are more appropriate to his own. (On the other hand, of course, it is possible that the children will not be content with standards which the teacher might accept if he were doing the job himself!) However, if the teacher can restrain himself from actually doing the work for the group, his own enthusiasm may well communicate itself to the children.

Probably the best starting point for successful group work is a topic or problem that has caught the children's own interests. This does not mean that the teacher can begin a group-work lesson by announcing that his pupils can do what they like, or can choose what interests them. Very often children find it extremely difficult to say what does interest them, especially if they are used to a teaching situation in which little regard has been paid previously to their tastes. They may be plunged into a state of anxiety by this sudden and unexpected call on their inward resources. Or they may well be reluctant to reveal their interests, even if they know them; perhaps because they are suspicious of a trick, perhaps because they resent an invasion of their privacy. Or the prospect of being responsible for their own ideas may itself make them feel inadequate.

This is a time when the teacher's skill and resourcefulness are called upon. From his knowledge of the individual members of his class, of their hobbies and out-of-school activities, of their conversations both in and out of the classroom, and especially of what has aroused their interest on previous occasions, the teacher should have a general idea of the kind of topic or problem which is likely to involve them. It may be that he is sufficiently confident of its appeal to be able to suggest a topic at the outset, being prepared to elaborate upon it if necessary. On the other hand, he may prefer to lead the class to arrive at the topic itself, through discussion and questions. If he does the latter, he should be sensitive to the mood of the class and be prepared to modify his suggestion if it does not meet with complete acceptance.

This initial discussion is a highly critical time for the success of the group work. In conducting it, the teacher must learn when to allow children to have their say, even if their contribution appears irrelevant, and when to summarize and formulate ideas which have been expressed only vaguely. Children are quick to feel snubbed and to withdraw into a protective shell of apathy or even hostility if their ideas are too readily dismissed. This is the more so when they offer those ideas hesitantly and shyly, perhaps relinquishing their defensive pose of passive and resigned compliance and instead exposing their inward selves for the first time in the classroom. Moreover, most children, while oversensitive themselves, will be the first to ride rough-shod over each other's ideas, scornfully drawing attention to their shortcomings without regard to the feelings of their proposers. It is the teacher's job to see that all members of the class get a fair hearing, and that their suggestions are seen in the most favourable light possible. This does not mean, of course, that their drawbacks should be ignored.

Another difficulty is that children may be overcome by the difficulty of formulating their ideas clearly and it is very easy for good ideas to get lost in vagueness and imprecision, with an attendant sense of frustration and futility. Children get frustrated easily and if the teacher does not tie the loose ends of a drawn-out discussion together and summarize its main points clearly, the class may relapse into a state of bored indifference.

Thus the teacher must tread a narrow path between the need to give opportunity for full discussion of ideas, and the need to give a sense of purpose and progress. He must avoid imposing his own ideas unless there is a complete dearth of suggestions from the class, and he must ensure that no contributions are given less than full attention. On the other hand, he must be prepared to make suggestions when none are forthcoming, such suggestions being based on his understanding of what ideas are likely to appeal to the class in question. Having made them, he must be prepared to modify them.

The question of the feasibility of proposed schemes is another important matter. There is clearly little point in elaborating plans for some activity which is simply not feasible. However, the teacher should beware of condemning proposals too readily on the grounds of their apparent unfeasibility. If a scheme which has fired the children's enthusiasm seems at first sight to be impracticable, the teacher should make every effort to see whether the difficulties involved in carrying it out cannot in fact be overcome, before he rules it out. Problems which appear intractable may well disappear in the face of a determination to resolve them. And even if it proves in the end that the practical difficulties involved are too great for the scheme to be implemented, the teacher will have gained the confidence of the class by demonstrating his sincerity in his attempt to overcome them.

DIFFERENT APPROACHES TO GROUP WORK

There must come a time when sufficient preliminary discussion has taken place for the proposals to have been fully aired, their advantages and drawbacks noted, and their feasibility agreed upon. Now is the time for the children to choose. There are two possible group-work situations within which they might be choosing. One is a topic which will involve the whole class, and groups are formed to tackle different aspects of it. The other is a series of different topics, and groups are formed in relation to these topics. In both situations the children are called upon to make a choice.

The first situation—one in which the whole class is pursuing a common topic—is nearly always the more fruitful, though it is at the same time the more difficult to organize. The children have in fact to make two choices: the whole class has to choose what topic to pursue, and then each child has to choose which aspect of the topic he wishes to help with. The choice of topic must be made democratically and it is important that it should be a realistic choice—that is, that all the alternatives are in fact possible. For this reason, any which have been deemed impracticable (after careful consideration) should be excluded, and if there are qualifications which the teacher feels it necessary to make regarding any of the proposals, these should be made clear beforehand. Voting may be by show of hands or secret ballot, but whichever it is, it should be conducted in a proper and serious manner, appropriate to the occasion. And, of course, it is essential for the teacher's future relations with the class that he does not begin to bring up objections to a scheme once it has been chosen.

It may be possible to specify the various tasks straight away, in which case the groups can be formed there and then. Experience suggests, however, that time spent in considering the division of the topic into its component aspects is seldom wasted. This may be done in class discussion, or if there are a number of alternative approaches to the topic, working parties may be formed to consider them, and to report back to the class with their advantages and disadvantages listed, and recommendations regarding their adoption. There is a drawback to the use of working parties to consider alternative approaches, however, and it is that the members of each working party may become so committed to the particular method they are examining that they become reluctant to abandon it when the time comes for reporting back. A similar difficulty arises when preliminary groups are formed to work out suggestions for a dramatic performance or display. It is because group work involves its participants in a way they are not involved in teacher-directed activities, that they become committed to what they are doing. The teacher must therefore use his discretion in deciding whether or not to form working parties, and how much time they should spend in preliminary discussions.

Once the general approach is decided upon, the different tasks appropriate to it can be determined and it is in relation to these that the groups are formed. As has been said before, it is essential that pupils are allowed complete freedom to choose which of these groups to join. However, this is often easier said than done. A necessary preliminary is that the pupils understand clearly what they are choosing from, and it is the teacher's job here to delineate as clearly as he can what the task of each group will be. At the same time, he must be careful not to prescribe the method of working, since this must rest with the group itself. As has been already suggested, the teacher may also help to make a child's choice meaningful by reminding him of his own interests and out-of-school activities, though the teacher should only do so if the child seems unable to make up his mind, and he should be careful not to try and influence his choice. Thus a boy may wish to act in a dramatic production and for this reason may elect to join the cast. It would be improper of the teacher to try to persuade him to join the production group, simply because he is known to be a good electrician.

The alternative situation in group work from that in which the whole class attempts a common topic is that in which a number of topics are pursued simultaneously by different groups. The organization of this is much easier and the teacher's role is simply that of making sure that the pupils understand clearly what each topic consists of before they choose. The topics may be those suggested by the teacher, or they may be suggested by the class. It is desirable that the topics should have some common element linking them. A situation in which a number of groups are pursuing totally unrelated activities is one in which there can be little opportunity for groups to learn from each other by exchanging information, and it is in the mutual exchange and evaluation of information and methods that some of the most valuable educational by-products of group work are to be gained.

Thus the teacher's role in specifying the task of the groups—that is, the group work itself—is both critical and difficult. He must make the specifications clear enough to ensure that each child can make a meaningful choice, without at the same time making them so prescriptive as to inhibit the group's initiative. And in the preliminary discussions he must give every contributor a fair hearing without allowing the impetus of the discussion to be lost through vagueness or irrelevance.

THE FORMATION OF THE GROUPS: SOCIOMETRY

The subject of group formation merits a book to itself and indeed, there is a whole library concerned with one particular method of forming groups—that of sociometry, devised by J. L. Moreno.[1] Basically, sociometry is a simple device for discovering and analysing patterns of mutual acceptance and rejection of each other by individuals in relation to proposed activities. It consists of getting each member of a group (in our case the whole class) to list in order of preference those other members with whom he would like to work, and the members with whom he does not wish to work. There are two important conditions which the sociometrician insists upon. Firstly, the listing of likes and dislikes must be seen to be secret. That is, the individual child making his list must be convinced that it is not going to be seen by any other member of the class. Secondly, the listing must be in relation to a specific and non-hypothetical activity. That is, each child must expect that, as a result of his listing, he will *in fact* find himself working with one or more of his preferences, and not with any of those whom he has rejected.

From these lists it is possible to construct sociograms (diagrams) or sociomatrices (tables) showing the pattern of preferences and rejections in a vivid form, and these may be used to form groups according to given principles—for example, that no group should contain any member who has been rejected by any other member, or that groups should contain the maximum number

[1] Moreno (1934).

possible of mutual choices. However, it is very easy to spend a great deal of time juggling with sociometric data and it may be doubted whether such time is justified for group work in the classroom. To be fair to sociometry, the main concern of the technique is to provide the data for the light they throw on interpersonal relationships; that groups are actually formed as a result is a by-product, though a by-product made necessary by the second of the two conditions mentioned above.

Apart from the time it takes, there are other disadvantages to the use of sociometry in forming groups in the classroom; in particular that it does not provide easily for alternative choices between different activities and—more important—it does not allow the pupils to know each other's choice. We have said above that there are two main factors likely to determine each child's preference: the nature of the group work, and the other children choosing that work. Both seem to us legitimate grounds on which to base a choice. To argue that children should choose solely on the basis of the work itself, and without regard to whom they will be working with, is as limited as it is unrealistic. We know very well that the attitude and personality of our own colleagues is an important contributory factor to the success of any undertaking we may engage upon, and this is at least as true if not more so of children.

From this it will be seen that we feel that sociometry, though a useful diagnostic and analytical tool, is not the most suitable way of forming groups for group work. However in skilled hands it may enable the teacher to anticipate certain problems and we would certainly not wish to be dogmatic on this point.[1]

PROBLEMS IN FORMING GROUPS

From what we have said above it follows that the machinery for forming groups should allow time and opportunity for the pupils not only to express their own choices, but also to see what

[1] A good textbook on the use of sociometry in the classroom is that by Gronlund (1959). A recent critical evaluation of sociometry in education has been made by Evans (1962).

choices others are making, and, if necessary, be able to alter their own in consequence. It will be appreciated that this requirement envisages a good deal of flexibility in the provisions for group formation and, indeed, flexibility may be said to be the keynote of the successful operation. Children will want to discuss with each other various possibilities and the wise teacher will give them the chance to do so. A number of difficulties may be foreseen, some real, some less important than they may seem at first sight.

One real difficulty is that some of the alternatives offered may be generally less popular than others, with the result that some groups may end up undersubscribed while others have too many members for their effective working. This brings us to the question of what size the groups should be—something that has not so far been considered. Obviously, the optimum size varies according to the purpose of the group. However, one can begin from the principle that every group should be large enough to ensure sufficient members for the carrying out of its task, and small enough to enable every member to contribute effectively. Three members is a basic minimum; more than eight is usually too many. From four to six members is about right for most activities; this provides for the division of labour within the group, and at the same time makes it reasonably likely that every member will participate in group discussions and decisions.

The problem of the oversubscription of some groups can always be better dealt with by anticipating it than after the event. With a little ingenuity, the teacher can often bring out in his specification of the work the less evident attractions of those activities which he suspects will not prove popular at first sight. He may think it desirable to fix an upper limit on the number of members of some or all the groups; if so, he should do this beforehand. And he should make sure that the sum of the maxima for all the groups is larger than the total number of children in the class, otherwise he is effectively limiting their freedom of choice. Another possibility is to subdivide overpopular aspects of the work into two or more activities, each of which can then become the province of its own group.

A different problem from that of the popular topic is that of the unpopular child, with whom nobody wants to work, the 'rejectee' in the jargon of sociometry. He may be unwanted by the others for a variety of reasons, some valid, some whimsical. Nonetheless, he must be allowed to choose like all the rest, and his choice—whatever motives the teacher may suspect it is based on—must be equally respected. The problem of the unwanted child is one of the reasons why the group-work teacher is well advised to try to keep the actual formation of the groups in a fairly fluid state at first. It is also another reason for not keeping the total allowed maximum numbers of the groups the same as the total in the class.

The timing of the placing of unwanted children in the groups of their choice is important. If an unpopular child chooses a group at an early stage in the formation of groups, the other children may avoid that group, changing their preferences to do so. On the other hand, the teacher must avoid at all costs the situation where most groups have been formed, and all that remains is to place an unpopular child. The announcement of his preference may well be met with expressions of protest from those already in the group, and the sense of group identity may lead them to make these protests more strongly than they really intend. The well-meaning teacher might then be led to suggest to the unfortunate rejectee that he might make another choice, whereupon that group, taking their cue from the others, will be even louder in their protestations.

'We don't want him! Why should we have to put up with him if that lot doesn't have to?'

However justified the reasons may be for his unpopularity, we have no right to expose a child to this sort of experience. The best time to allow unwanted children to make their choice is about halfway through the process of forming the groups, when each group has enough foundation members for his addition not to put the rest off joining it, but has not yet reached that stage of group identification which might lead to protests about the new member.

The problems of overpopular topics and unwanted children present real difficulties in the formation of groups through free choice. Other difficulties which are often pointed out, but which in fact rarely prove so grave as might be supposed, are the danger that known troublemakers might get together in one group in order to play the teacher up, and the possibility that skills and talents in the class may not be found in the groups where they might be best employed.

The advice, 'Find the troublemakers and separate them,' is probably as old as class-teaching. In the context of teacher-directed activities it is good advice, provided that we recognize that in carrying it out we are dealing with a symptom of the disease, rather than with the disease itself—the disease in question being nearly always boredom. But in the context of group work, the same precept may well prove inapplicable. The co-operative energy that was devoted to tiresome tricks may now be put to the solution of the problem facing the group. A good deal of difficult behaviour in class is in fact rebellion against being made to do something the child has no wish to do. Because in group work he has freely chosen what to do, he may no longer feel any need to rebel. Very often two or more recognized troublemakers may take the opportunity afforded by group work to show the other children—and the teacher—that they are in fact more hard-working, more imaginative and indeed altogether more able than the rest of the class put together. Fired by this some-what ignoble motive, they may well surprise both their fellows and themselves by what they do in fact achieve.

Needless to say, group work does not work miracles. But it is surprising how often teachers will comment on the changed attitudes of troublesome children after they have taken part in a successful piece of group work. We believe this to be so for two reasons. Firstly the child is not being compelled to perform a task he judges to be irrelevant to his own interests, and secondly he is free to control the direction of his own efforts.

The other objection sometimes raised to the formation of groups by free choice is that it is not always compatible with the efficient division of labour. Children with particular talents

GWSS—C

may elect not to join those groups in which their talents would be put to best use. Two counter-arguments may be raised to this objection. The first is that children, like adults, normally enjoy doing what they are good at and far from not ending up in those groups in which their talents would be most usefully employed, are more likely to choose those groups for the very reason that they can employ their talents in them. The second counter-argument is far more cogent, and is based on the principle fundamental to group work already stated: that the value of any group-work activity is assessed, not in terms of the quality of the end-product, but in terms of the contribution that each child has put into its production. Seen from the teacher's point of view, the actual end-product itself is a secondary consideration; he is primarily concerned with what the child has gained in producing it. In this respect, the end-product is like an artist's working sketch, which is discarded once it has served its purpose. The group work itself may be imperfect and full of mistakes. The teacher knows that the children who produced the work have in fact learnt from those mistakes. Thus it may be more profitable for a child to be allowed to join a group in which undeveloped skills are exercised, than for him to take part in an activity in which a highly developed skill is put to use. In the first case he may learn something new; in the second, he may only derive pleasure from doing something he can already do well.

It should be appreciated by now that the actual formation of the groups is a critical matter. It should be firmly based, and moreover *seen* to be based, on the pupils' freedom of choice. At the same time, the teacher should endeavour to ensure that the groups are neither too large nor too small, and that they do not contain members who have been explicitly rejected by the others.

The reader may complain that this advice seems to be contradictory. If children are to be allowed freedom of choice, then unless their preferences happen to fall within the predetermined limits, any attempt to increase or decrease the sizes of groups must be an infringement of some child's expressed wish. But in fact this difficulty can be dealt with, provided the teacher makes clear beforehand any limitations he may think necessary, and provided he keeps the actual formation of groups in a fluid situation until he has seen that their sizes are appropriate to their tasks. One method of anticipating difficulties arising from the overpopularity of some groups is for the teacher to ask children to make more than one choice. In such cases, it may be wise to ask them to indicate whether their first choice is based on very strong preference, or whether they are quite prepared to be moved if some groups prove too large. On the other hand, if certain activities are in fact heavily undersubscribed, the teacher might do better to ask himself whether the children are going to benefit from undertaking them at all.

THE GROUP PROCEDURE

The manner in which the members of the group carry out their joint task is important to the success of group work as an educational experience. On the other hand, this is an area in which too much direction on the part of the teacher may well invalidate the whole purpose of the exercise. It is a principle of group work that children learn from their mistakes, and this applies as much to the actual running of the group, as to the work itself. Nevertheless, suggestions from the teacher before the actual work begins, and preferably before the groups are formed, are necessary if the children are unused to working in this way. In giving them, the teacher should himself be prepared to accept modifications in practice, even though he may think it wise to be quite explicit at first, in order to help the groups get started.

There are three main ways in which a group can undertake the work in hand: by choosing a leader, or accepting a self-appointed one, and following out his instructions; by each individual member marking out a particular aspect of the work for himself and then embarking upon it, with varying degrees of consultation with his fellows; or by the groups agreeing on a division of labour through preliminary discussion. These three methods may be described as authoritarian, *laissez faire* and democratic.[1]

[1] Using the terms of the classic experiments by Lippitt and White; see pp. 88 *et seq.* below.

Which of these three approaches is thought best depends to a
very large extent upon what is thought to be the main aim of the
group work. If the success of any particular undertaking is to be
assessed in relation to the quality of the end-product, then the
authoritarian method probably provides the framework with the
greatest potential for its achievement, though it does not necessarily follow that a group run in this way will in fact produce a
successful outcome. This must depend very much on the personality and vision of the leader, and on the capacity for being led
by the rest of the group. And in activities in which artistic imagination is a central factor, such as dramatic performances and
displays, an inspired leader may enable the group to produce
work of a very much higher order than might have been the
outcome of co-operative effort. (The inspired leader is not only
effective in artistic productions; Joyce Cary's delightful novel
Mister Johnson[1] gives a vivid and convincing account of how
a self-appointed leader can imbue even a mundane activity like
road-digging with a chiliastic note.)

However, it has already been declared as a principle of group
work that the quality of the end-product is less important than
the quality of the members' individual contributions and for this
reason if no other the teacher should be chary of encouraging
groups to adopt an authoritarian procedure. This is not to say that
the end-product is of no consequence. Indeed, we would argue
that the sense of real achievement that can be obtained from
working in this way towards a satisfactory conclusion is of value
in itself. What we would stress, however, is that there should be
no distortion on the part of the teacher in order to achieve what
he conceives to be a satisfactory end or conclusion. On the other
hand, if there is a natural leader in a group, it is generally better
that he should become the group's chairman than that he should
become its director, since in the former role he may well devote
some of his energy to seeing that all members of the group have
their say.

The *laissez-faire* method of group procedure may well at first

---

[1] Cary (1947).

seem the least satisfactory. However, with a small group of, say, three or four members, the line between *laissez-faire* and democratic procedure may be difficult to draw; individuals may be working under a sort of tacit-agreement principle. Moreover, to insist on formal discussion and voting may be distasteful to some teachers, though it may be noted that very often groups formed by children for their own purposes—clubs, and secret societies, for instance—often rejoice in elaborate rules of democratic procedure, and the teacher who dispenses with voting on the grounds that the pupils will be bored by it should be sure that he is not projecting his own feelings in the matter.

It may be inferred from the preceding paragraphs that we feel that the democratic approach is generally to be preferred, and this is in keeping with the principle that it is in the child's contribution rather than in the end-product that the main value of group work lies. A group that proceeds by discussion and agreed decisions is one in which each individual may be expected to participate to the full, and one from which he may be expected to derive the greatest educational benefit. And it may be noted in passing that in the phrase 'educational benefit' we include the acquisition of new knowledge and the effective handling of it, as well as the learning of the skills upon which democracy depends: the ability to co-operate, the ability to define problems and formulate plans of action, as well as the ability to evaluate their success. Children who undertake some activity of their own free will and on the basis of co-operative effort are more likely to retain the attendant information than children who are directed to it.

Democratic procedure, then, is to be preferred, and it is perhaps a sad reflection on our society that it may have to be spelled out to some children. The teacher should explain both the need for a chairman, and his role, and in describing the latter he should stress the point that it is a chairman's responsibility to see that every member of the group has an opportunity to voice his opinion to the others. All children should have the opportunity of acting as chairmen, though with inexperienced group workers it may be wise to allow the natural leaders to fulfil this role on a number of occasions before insisting on a rota.

Each group should keep a record of its decisions, and this should include details of job responsibilities within the group. This performs the double purpose of constituting a reference in disputes, and providing the teacher with a means of keeping a check on the group's progress. The nature of the record will naturally vary with the activity, but it should include as a minimum details of the plan of work, and a progress report for each lesson.

THE AVAILABILITY OF MATERIALS AND FACILITIES

One of the requirements of group work which the teacher often learns the hard way is the need for an early estimate of materials, equipment, apparatus and other provisions that will have to be made in advance. It is our experience that one of the commonest causes of the failure of promising undertakings is that of leaving these matters until too late. This is particularly important where activities entail contacts outside the school, such as visits to factory premises, newspaper offices or other such places, which may have to be booked months ahead. Even such public institutions as museums may require advance notice of a visit by a party, and in any case it is often necessary to have at least seven days' notice of an outside visit in order to arrange transport.

Specialized pieces of equipment may take many weeks before they arrive, and there may be need to secure special approval of the order itself, which will add to the delay. In this respect, teachers would do well to consider whether it would not be possible—and more valuable—for the children to make such equipment themselves. However, even paper and other common materials take time to obtain.

Thus the experienced teacher makes sure that when proposals for group-work schemes are being considered, a preliminary estimate of their requirements in terms of materials, apparatus and other outgoings is drawn up before they are voted upon, and it may be that considerations of supply or expense constitute a valid reason for disallowing them. Though here again the teacher should not disallow a proposal from a superficial assessment of supply difficulties; one alternative is to suggest that the proposers think of other ways of achieving the same result by different means.

All this does not mean that the teacher himself should undertake all the necessary ordering, arranging of visits, and so forth. Wherever possible, the members of the group concerned should be expected to draw up their own estimates and write letters concerned with visits; the incidental consultation of catalogues, timetables and other reference books is an important source of learning. This is one area, however, where the teacher will probably want to check plans before they are acted upon, if only for the sake of the school funds and the school's reputation with outside bodies. While it is true that in group work children learn from their own mistakes, it is unfair to expect anyone outside the classroom to put up with their outcome.

THE EVALUATION OF PROGRESS

This brings us to a consideration of how the teacher keeps a check on the progress of individual children. We would ourselves argue that, ideally, there is no need for individuals' progress to be recorded; since the children are co-operating in groups, the logical unit of assessment is the group itself. And furthermore, since we are concerned to engender a self-reliant and self-critical attitude, we would argue for the ultimate abandonment of any form of assessment other than the groups' own progress reports. However, it must be admitted that in the short term the teacher's demand for some kind of check on the individual pupil's progress is a reasonable one, if only as a means of judging the value of group work itself, and here we may usefully kill two birds with one stone by suggesting that the teacher who feels ill at ease doing nothing while his class is busily occupied could well spend some of the time in recording the progress made by each individual. Such a record of progress might include a check list of skills, techniques, procedures and areas of factual knowledge which it is intended that the pupil should cover. Then the individual progress record can consist of numbered and dated entries, with a cross reference from the check list to the reference number of the entry in which evidence of the relevant skill or whatever was shown. The teacher will have to give thought beforehand to the best way in which the group records should be kept, to enable him to keep a check on the contribution of each individual member without imposing artificial restraints on something which is, after all, a co-operative venture. He will also want to spend time with each group in turn, contributing to their discussions, asking questions where it seems to him that important matters are being overlooked, being ready with suggestions but sparing in their utterance and giving advice only when it seems to him that the group itself is unable to arrive at the answers through its own efforts. During these periods of participation, he will be unobtrusively observing the group as a co-operating whole, noting the interaction of its members, and the contribution of individuals. Afterwards he may wish to record these observations himself. Though it should be noted that, with individual records as well as with the records of group activities, the more that these records can form part of the work of the group, and therefore be done by the members of the group themselves, the more reliable they are likely to be. What the teacher sees is, after all, likely to be only a small part of the work and progress of any individual.

It must be emphasized, however, that the aim of group work goes well beyond that of providing an alternative method of covering a traditional syllabus, though we would insist that it is possible to cover most areas of such syllabuses provided the teacher plans over a long period (say a minimum of a year's work), and provided he is prepared for his pupils to deal with the topics in the order in which they arise, and not necessarily according to the order on the syllabus. Moreover, we would claim that once a topic has been dealt with in the process of group work, it will prove to have been learnt much more effectively and certainly much more meaningfully than in traditional class teaching, though we would also agree that there are probably areas in every syllabus which do not lend themselves to the group-work approach.

PROVISION FOR REPORTING BACK

Since group work has some expressed aim other than that simply of giving the pupils an opportunity to learn the topics involved (though that may be the teacher's main purpose in embarking upon it), it is important that there should be proper and clear machinery for the group to make its findings known. The form in which this is to be done may well be part of the specification; for example, in drawing a plan or map, in putting on a masque, or in staging an exhibition, the manner of presentation is implicit in the specification. In other cases, however, the manner in which the outcome of the group's activities is reported back may not be implicit in the work itself, as, for instance, in a survey or investigation. With children who are used to group work, the teacher may prefer to leave the devising of the most effective means of reporting to the initiative of the group itself, but with beginners it is better to include the recommended form of reporting back in the specification of the work, so that the children have a clear idea of what they are working towards. In deciding upon the most suitable means of reporting, one should always have regard to the audience for whom the report is intended, and the purpose of the report, as well as to its contents. Exhibitions and displays may be a more effective method of presenting the group's findings than in a closely written document; on the other hand, if the record is to be used for reference purposes, it may be better to have it in a semi-permanent form, such as that provided by a file. And, in passing, we would draw attention to the fact that drama, though now largely intended as a form of entertainment, started out as a means of instructing, and is still so used today by the aborigines of Australia. (In his novel *Voss*, Patrick White gives an instance of how an aboriginal corroboree is used to record an important incident in the life of the tribe.[1]) Given encouragement and appreciation, children will readily devise more imaginative and effective means of presenting their group findings than the familiar decorated folder.

[1] White (1957).

This brings us to our final piece of advice in group-work methods generally. The teacher should take the opportunity of making the reporting back of groups something of a special event. The readers of Sybil Marshall's delightful book, *An Experiment in Education*, will remember Roger, the educationally retarded boy who spent a month behind the piano in the classroom, making a huge paper mosaic. Mrs. Marshall had promised Roger that she would not look at the mosaic until it was finished, and in order for him to have the necessary privacy she had—at his suggestion—pulled the piano away from one of the walls. Every day for the best part of a month Roger worked away at his picture until the time came for it to be seen. Mrs. Marshall knew that this was an important occasion in Roger's life and, within the limitations of a country classroom, she treated it as such. She suspended the work of the whole class and then turned her back and looked out of the window while Roger arranged two chairs and got two of his friends to hold the finished mosaic—which measured forty by thirty inches—up between them. Then he stood beside his handiwork and told her he was ready. We may imagine her expression of genuine wonder and delight when she turned round as we look at the colour reproduction in her book and remember that the original was produced by a boy of eleven with a very bad squint who, at seven, had been 'little better than an uneducatable idiot.'[1]

When children have invested their emotions as well as their energies in a piece of work, the teacher should recognize this by treating its presentation as something of an occasion. At the same time, they should be chary of making this a *public* occasion. As has been said before, the value of group work derives from what the children get out of it, not from the end-product. The teacher would be well advised, therefore, to resist the temptation to exhibit the work produced further than to the class itself, otherwise there is a real danger of too great a concentration on its merits as an item for display, and not enough on its value as part of an educational process.

[1] Marshall (1963) p. 62 and Plate 19.

5 *Group work in action*

In the present chapter are outlined some examples of group work, based upon the writers' own experience and upon the students' work. These examples have been chosen to illustrate particular points and are not given here as necessarily constituting procedures to be imitated in detail.

INTRODUCING THE METHOD:
A DEVELOPMENT OF CO-OPERATIVE WORKING

With group work an important problem is not so much thinking of topics that may be of interest, but deciding the appropriateness of the work and topics at the stage already reached by the children who are to be involved. Particularly is this so if we accept the importance of freedom and individual contribution at all stages including the earliest. Some thought also needs to be given to the way in which the children have been used to working previously. Where they have been used to more formal work which has been mainly teacher-controlled, and in which each stage in the work has been arrived at by the teacher beforehand in his own lesson preparation and planning, the new freedoms may well lead to groups trying to undertake tasks beyond their ability to organize. This will inevitably lead to unnecessary frustrations and possibly to a breakdown in the internal organization of the group, with the result that investigations will not be successfully conducted, the overall standards will fall and the effort will be meaningless. The children themselves will quickly recognize this situation, and will reject the method, which will become devalued in their eyes. At best it will become merely an occasion for drawing and copying long passages from text books which will serve no useful purpose from the point of view of an exercise of inquiry or extension of knowledge and experience; at worst, the whole episode may develop into chaos.

One method successfully used with third-year secondary children who have been used to direct-teaching methods was to invite each individual child in the class to choose a topic which was to form the basis of a piece of individual investigation. It was pointed out by the teacher concerned that he appreciated that each child had his or her own particular interests and that he would like to widen the scope of their work in school so as to include more time for them to follow up these lines. Direct class teaching was then used in order to outline, in a very simple way, methods by which the children could follow a line of investigation by:

1. deciding upon a topic or question;
2. using the school and public library, together with other books, magazines and sources to collect information;
3. contacting individuals or associations who could give further information and making visits themselves, in their own time for the same purpose;
4. presenting their findings in written, pictorial and graph form (according to the type of information);
5. arriving at some conclusions, however tentative, based upon what they had themselves discovered.

Children were given a week in which to decide for themselves what they wanted to do, and time was allocated during the following week for the teacher and pupils to discuss, individually, some of the plans.

Inevitably standards varied, but on the whole the children welcomed the chance to use their private interests and pet hobbies as part of their school work. Added to which the demands, although new enough to create interest, were not so far divorced from their earlier experiences associated with writing 'compositions'. No particular time limit was set, but a double period was devoted to the activity each week and it was agreed to 'see what had happened' in a month's time. The topic list was varied but, as one might have expected, continued to reflect the more conventional work done in other subjects, particularly history and geography. Many of the choices were associated with each other and this, later, gave scope for co-operation, although initially each child worked individually. Even so, there were at the outset some individuals who welcomed the opportunity to follow their own interests. One boy chose to write on pigeon-keeping, another began with an account of how he had bought some hens with money earned on his paper round, and finally concluded with a thoroughgoing account, including costs, prices, and egg sales, of his 'chicken farm'. Another, fired with accounts of the activities of John Howard and Elizabeth Fry, began with the history of prison reform and finished with a thoughtful analysis of present day juvenile delinquency as he saw it, in which he included some case studies of acquaintances that society had classed as delinquents.

From time to time, individuals would present 'papers' to the rest, telling of what they were doing and how they were working. Periodically a radio or television broadcast would have some bearing on one or other of the topics and the teacher would recommend the person to whom it seemed relevant to listen. In this way the children began to widen their spheres of contact for information. It was not long before individuals began to pass relevant findings from their own work to their friends engaged upon some other activity.

After a few weeks, by which time new topics had been started and children had grown much more accustomed to the methods, two groups of pupils suggested that they should work together on one particular topic—'because we can find out more if we work together'. The suggestion was readily accepted by the teacher and it was found that others also wanted to work in this way. One group wanted to investigate the history of a nearby village, which had an old abbey and evidence of early settlement near the school itself, while the other set about an investigation into the development and present output of a large aircraft company situated about two miles from the school which gave employment to a significant number of people living in the vicinity. Other groups of children combined to make their own contributions.

This example is quoted to show how the children developed the idea of co-operative effort in an endeavour to pool their resources as they discovered that they could in fact benefit from so doing. The original idea was introduced by the teacher, growing out of more conventional working methods, and was taken up and expanded successfully by the children themselves.

Another form of co-operative enterprise involving group work, but which does not follow the same lines as that already given in that it has considerably more limited objective, is that of producing a class newspaper. Such an activity can profitably be linked with direct teaching or individual and group methods and can begin with newspaper comparison. We have often found that third-, fourth- and fifth-year secondary children are surprised to find that what makes news for one paper is barely mentioned in another, and also that some news items are reported in an almost identical manner in each paper. A study that begins with a period of newspaper comparisons is striking in itself, particularly if the choice is carefully made to show contrasts. Situations involving subjective and objective reporting of incidents can be engineered in the classroom and outside of it, for everyone tends to see things differently. Groups of children with similar interests can be combined as reporters, and an editor and his assistant can make the final selection if the contributions are too numerous. School concerts, sports and other activities may form subjects for inclusion, together with other items of interest including interviews with staff members, criticisms of T.V., plays and school rules. And there should also be scope for wider reporting, beyond the school itself.

Activities of this kind may well have a limited duration and are best abandoned when interest flags. The main value, apart from comparisons of national dailies mentioned earlier, is that children are writing commentaries on events as they occur, are observing, balancing and presenting information; this in turn seems to lead to a greater appreciation of the nature of 'news'.

THEMATIC GROUP WORK:
AN OUTLINE OF A WORKING SCHEME

An important aspect of group work is that it enables the children to become directly involved with the information, knowledge and ideas that they themselves are using. For this very reason, the amount of effort called for on the part of the teacher is considerably greater than that involved in more formal situations, when the teacher collects the information and presents it to a passive audience. Because of this it is necessary for the framework, within which the main body of the work is to be carried out, to be constructed coherently and in such a way that the teacher can, in fact, plan ahead. We would certainly not advocate that any teacher, however competent, should merely arrive at his class, devoid of ideas, to ask thirty youngsters: 'What do you want to do today?'

The democracy and pupil-involvement in group work are gained through the teacher and pupils planning together what will happen during the ensuing weeks. The feasibility of ideas must be considered by both together and either incorporated or rejected by the pupils. The flexibility of the scheme must be in its inner workings rather than in its overall agreed framework. The children themselves welcome such an arrangement and it is our experience that they will co-operate readily when they know what is involved provided that they have agreed to it and that their own contributions have been included. Indeed, they welcome the stability of the framework because they know what they are trying to do.

In this connection, some teachers work on thematic lines. A theme or continuing idea with many associated aspects may be taken and followed for a whole term or even longer. One very important value of this kind of approach is that it can lead to the co-operation of a number of subject departments, thus contributing to the idea of unity of all knowledge, reducing ideas of compartmentalization and subject-divisions in the minds of the children who are working in the field.

The authors have been practically involved with children in a number of such themes, one of which is outlined below.

A class of adolescents were particularly anxious to raise some money towards the school contribution to Oxfam, but wanted to know more about the work of that organization. Discussion in the classroom led to a variety of views about why Britain did not suffer from the same kinds of disease and calamity that befell some countries. Discussion ranged widely until it was suggested that we should run a course on health, and why other countries were so poor. It was as vague as that to begin with. We set about planning the 'course' together. We decided we would begin with this country and ourselves, examine our health services, and then look at other countries and see why things were going wrong elsewhere. It was accepted that Britain was a rich, industrial country with roads, houses, an educational system and resources to provide and maintain them. We decided that we would divide into groups of five or six and choose topics of interest to follow up, following talks, films and visits connected with the subject.

Thus we began with children and their needs, including foods such as proteins, vitamins and carbohydrates. The school health and dental services, medical services, voluntary services, the National Health, Insurance and Pension Services, were looked at. Speakers came with films from the nursing services; a dentist, a doctor, a public health inspector, all made contributions and the groups followed up aspects of the work they did. This covered a whole term's work and had involved us in visits to a blood transfusion unit, the local docks, and to a food processing plant. Now we looked outward. The British representative to an F.A.O. conference came and answered questions on world food supply and distribution, as did representatives of other countries, particularly from the Commonwealth.

Meanwhile the children themselves worked in groups on particular aspects, some on school health, others on young children's needs. One group investigated world food supplies and another presented information on the World Health Organization and U.N.I.C.E.F.

The weekly study became a year's work and involved the science, history, geography, rural science and mathematics departments of the school.

The work undertaken by these groups was valuable in various ways. In the first place they were doing something that had arisen from their own interests. They were involved at all planning stages and directed their own work in groups. Individuals were free to follow their own lines of inquiry and since the subject area was directly related to human needs, they were personally involved. More than this, they could draw upon information that was available on a day-to-day basis through the medium of television, radio, newspaper as current news items all fell within the scope of their activity. Reports of drought, famine and flood, presented as news items, were interpreted in terms of their work and not as passing incidents of fleeting interest, lacking in real meaning. The fact that people who were themselves committed to work in aspects of the problems and to a particular viewpoint came, talked and mixed with the children, gave a validity to their own efforts and led to a more personal involvement on their own part. In brief, they became more personally concerned. The fact that they were looking outward beyond themselves and were free to follow lines of interest led to a development of new attitudes for themselves; they began to reject many of their earlier views and prejudices about their own country as well as others, questioning more and more, in an increasingly informed way, a world system that it seemed to require the existence of scarcity and deprivation for its own perpetuation.

Another important result of this method of working in this particular example, was the fact that there was a growing realization that nothing could be easily set aside as not being relevant. The dramatic chain reaction of ignorance, disease, unemployment, poverty was recognized and the formula was applied in varying degrees not only to the underdeveloped areas, but also to social groups at home. Terms such as 'good' and 'bad', hitherto easily applied to individual families within their own community, were dropped as the children's awareness increased and they became more discerning. Cause and effect began to take on a new significance, a situation that marked a new stage in intellectual growth.

This is a feature of group work that is particularly important. There is time for growth. The freedom within the situation provides the opportunity for the child to work along lines of his own interests within the overall scheme, whilst at the same time he has a responsibility to his colleagues to carry out the task and come up with results.

THE EFFECTS OF GROUP WORK
ON PUPILS' SOCIAL BEHAVIOUR

So far we have discussed group work as a part of the school activity and we have assumed that in most other respects of their daily lives, the children concerned have been subjected to formal teaching methods. We have, however, had the opportunity of operating a scheme over a period of several years in which it was applied in a wider context. This was in a boys' comprehensive school where group methods were applied over the whole of the fourth year and involved the children in a free choice of activities ranging from mountaineering to interior decorating. Although none of the activities was 'academic', nonetheless skills acquired in the normal classroom subjects were used and developed.

The main object was to help the groups integrate socially within the school itself. The need to do so arose directly as a result of what may loosely be described as 'growing discipline troubles', destructiveness, damage, bullying and rebellion against individual teachers and indeed authority as a whole. Discussion between some of the staff and pupils revealed that there was a feeling of growing unrest and dissatisfaction with 'book-learning'. Pupils felt their life from 9.0 a.m. to 4.0 p.m. was unrelated both to their life outside these hours and to what would be expected of them when they left school at the end of the year.

Full credit must be given to the school for the fact that the rebelliousness did not lead to an increase in punishments and sanctions, but that, instead, a hard, critical look was taken at the curriculum for the fourth-year classes mainly concerned.

In the event, the timetable was reorganized so that teachers with varied interests, who were flexible in their approach and sympathetic to the needs of these young people, were available to work with them at certain periods of the week and during the whole of one afternoon. At this point the pupils were consulted in groups and activities emerged under a number of headings including interior decorating, rock climbing, canoeing and swimming, photography, art, expeditions to include map-reading, hiking and visits of interest, motor maintenance, building, and drama. The pupils were given the chance to opt for any course, but they had to change over at the end of one and a half terms.

The effect was quite dramatic. Not only did the discipline troubles virtually cease, but also the boys' whole attitude to the school became more positive, and there was a marked improvement in the more conventional work still carried out in the classroom. The pupils both saw the practical concern of the school for them, and were themselves actively committed to the school. The school became a place wherein their recognized needs were met, instead of a place where they were bored.

One cannot dictate needs to others—these can only be felt by those concerned. No one is satisfied in receiving ministrations to an assumed but unfelt need, and yet this is just what we expect all too often of children. Such impositions on the part of school authority can result only in an enforced erosion of individuality through submissiveness, rejection and apathy, or rebellion on the part of the pupil.

GROUP WORK AND EXAMINATIONS

In Chapter I we quoted an excerpt from a conversation with children in a pre-examination class where, under the guidance of students, group-work methods had been used in a study of fuel and power. The topic formed part of the Certificate in Secondary Education examination syllabus and was carried out during February and March by four-year pupils who were sitting for the examination the following year. Direct-teaching methods were used in conjunction with the group work during a separate period in the week. By this arrangement it was possible to give general attention to certain basic principles and at the same time to give freedom to the pupils concerned to follow up their own lines of inquiry and application using practical examples. The main subject was electricity, and the direct teaching involved formally organized experiments, which were teacher-directed, dealing with voltage, wattage, how generators worked, and the main principles of electricity. The application of this information was through group work.

Following general discussion in which the class and students were involved, five sub-headings were agreed to cover the more important features of the manufacture and distribution of electricity in Britain. Pupils were then selected to work within one of the five main subdivisions, four in each group.

Group 1. The mining of coal for use in power stations.
Group 2. The North Sea Project.
Group 3. The National Grid System.
Group 4. Some domestic and industrial uses of electricity.
Group 5. New methods of producing electricity: nuclear power stations.

Visits to a main power station and to a sub-station where voltage was transformed for domestic distribution were arranged for all groups, and two films were shown to the whole class. Individual groups also incorporated and planned their own models and experiments as part of their work. The task covered nine weeks, with no extra time being allotted beyond the usual science periods.

By working in this way the pupils made more direct contact with sources of information and were selective in their use of the information they received. They chose what was relevant to the particular study and utilized it. More than this, they had to find out the sources of the information needed, and make the necessary approach, usually by letter. This in turn meant that they had to consider what it was that they wanted to know and to clarify their own ideas even before they could begin their inquiries. In so doing they were drawing upon earlier knowledge gained and were consolidating and extending it. They also discovered just where the gaps in their knowledge were; as one boy said in interview towards the end of the project: 'You come across things you don't know so you try to find out.' The motivation 'to try to find out' is all the greater where the finding out is a means to an end and not merely an end in itself.

We doubt whether any pupil taking part felt at the end that he knew all there is to know about electricity and power supply, and this is yet another important feature of working in this way. The realization that 'things are happening even when you're not studying them', is surely more realistic than the encouragement given to the idea of finality generated in all too many children when they have comprehensively 'done' a particular topic in a formal manner in a nice, tidy compartment.

The above is an example of where group methods were used prior to an examination. Another example illustrates how information given for examination purposes can be brought to life and applied in real situations in which children find themselves.

The end-of-year external examinations having finished, it was suggested to a fifth-year form by the geography teacher, that they should take a look at the place in which they lived and find out more about it. In this case the original idea emanated from the teacher. The conventional syllabus for examination purposes had included settlement, transport, natural resources, trade and the location of industry, and the use of Ordnance Survey maps, together with aspects of the economic geography of Europe. There had, however, been no attempt made at a detailed environmental study using some of the principles covered in the wider geography teaching.

As in the earlier examples quoted, there was a wide discussion of points that might well be considered in a question of this kind, and it was not altogether surprising that these adolescents were interested in the possibilities of such a study from particular viewpoints. What was interesting was that, from the outset, they expressed a strong desire to carry out the work from the social rather than from a narrower geographical point of view. They held opinions about their environment and these they wanted to test, although this was not the way in which it was expressed. Their study was not going to be a mere examination of patterns of local settlement.

They expressed their views, mainly on the inadequacies of the district, during the initial discussions. It became clear that these attitudes were motivating the children and influencing the structure their investigation was to take. Local industry and employment opportunities were criticized, as were transport to other areas of the city, and the provision and siting of local amenities. The view that there were 'too many people of the same kind' living in the area was also expressed by them.

It was evident that these were views children themselves wanted to test and this became the purpose of the project itself.

The investigation was divided under three broad headings, which could loosely be described as referring to social factors, economic factors and services. Individuals chose their groups freely on the basis of their views, interests and friends. Some changes took place on a minor scale so as to try to arrive at a balance between groups, but no pressure was exerted and people were left free to fit in as they wanted.

The next decision to be made, corporately, was how information was to be presented. The most appropriate way was thought to be by recording much of it in a large-scale drawing of the area, and a boundary was agreed, based upon the main roads surrounding the main catchment area of the school itself. Even this was open to question, and it was suggested that it might well be found that the boundaries should be flexible in the light of findings. Two children particularly interested in mapping and illustrations undertook to paint a scale map on a piece of plaster board some 4′ 6″ × 6′ 0″ and to plan a key for it.

Because of the particular views held about their environment, it was quickly decided to make a survey of occupations of parents of children attending the school itself, who were mainly drawn locally. Discussion within the class of twenty-five ranged around the best way to do this without duplicating answers and without causing undue embarrassment. Accepting that the information received would serve only as useful guide-lines, it was decided that each inquirer should ask three questions of five children at random in each form of the five-stream-entry school. This would give a total random survey of people in the school, and the school itself was one which virtually all boys in the designated area attended. The first question was to establish that the interviewee lived within the agreed boundary, the second: 'Have you a brother in school?' was designed to eliminate double counting. If the answer to this was in the affirmative, the inquirer did not proceed, but found a new subject. The last question, 'What is your father's job and firm?', was recorded if the first two questions were satisfactorily answered. No names were recorded. The method was crude, but it was what the children had themselves devised and later was criticized by themselves. Indeed the children included the following comment in their final report: 'We found some difficulty in dealing with the answers to the third question. We found that some of the answers given were so wide as to lead to doubt as to what the actual occupation classification should be. We found it difficult in a number of cases to decide, for example, whether an 'engineer' was skilled, semi-skilled or an unskilled factory worker. Any future survey should perhaps contain a larger number of alternative questions.' These words are taken from the final report made by the pupils themselves.

The occupational grades devised were managerial, clerical, skilled manual, unskilled manual, shop assistants, transport, deceased, unemployed, and 'don't know'. These titles were arrived at following the efforts of one of the groups to find the employment opportunities in the area, and as a result of their approach to local firms. Their information was fed back into the group as a whole and used by others.

Yet another extract from the final report shows the quality of the efforts and the critical level of work carried out by the children themselves: 'We did not find it necessary to create a new section. Although there are teachers living within the area and at least one doctor, they are not numerous enough to have any statistical significance in our sample.'

The other part of this particular survey showed that local firms were totally insignificant from the employment viewpoint. In fact no parent was employed by any of the locally-listed firms. When this point was examined by the groups there was some concern since the returns from the companies themselves showed they employed between them about six hundred workers, and that they judged that they did give employment to local labour. Since the two pieces of information did not correspond, pupils fell to arguing about the kinds of questions they had asked and finally arrived at the conclusion that the incidence of the numbers of people locally employed must have been small among fathers, but was greater among brothers, sisters and mothers, and some of them determined to find out if this was so.

The value of this particular exercise was that they were prepared to examine critically their own methods of working and standards of accuracy in the light of the limited information they already held whereas they might well have remained satisfied merely with the acquisition of the knowledge itself.

6 The rationale of group work

Group work as a teaching approach in secondary schools can be justified from the educational point of view on two main counts: first, that it is at least as efficient as traditional class teaching in many areas of the school curriculum; second, that its aims go beyond the limits of the academic syllabus to the field of social education, a vital part of the school's total responsibility. There are further considerations, but for the purposes of this chapter we shall confine ourselves to these two justifications, and work on the assumption that the group work in question is proceeding satisfactorily and along the lines we have suggested. Our task here, then, is to show what theoretical foundations group work is based upon.

THE PSYCHOLOGY OF PUBERTY AND ADOLESCENCE

We may begin from the psychology of the older child. The onset of puberty and the ensuing phase of adolescence is a stage of human development which is marked above all by uncertainty. Conscious of the physical changes which are taking place in his body, and aware of strange and sometimes disturbing emotions accompanying them, the normal pubescent child experiences a setback in what has been up to now an ever-increasing understanding and capacity for dealing with the world at large. His life-pattern so far has been characterized, perhaps all too slowly but nevertheless with apparent inevitability, by an increase in physical strength and powers of endurance, an increase in motor skills and manual dexterity, an increase in intellectual understanding and mental power, an increase in social control, as well as a demonstrable increase in mere size. Unless he has suffered a severe illness or has been in some way emotionally disturbed, his progress has been always in one direction. No doubt there have been minor setbacks, and no doubt occasions when he has experienced the frustration of his own limitations and a despair of ever achieving adulthood. But for the most part it has seemed that he has but to wait and he will comprehend everything and what is more, encompass everything. The small boy who announces: 'When I'm a man I shall be a king', the small girl who asserts: 'When I'm grown up, I shall be a famous ballet dancer', are each of them stating what they take to be no more than the simple truth, based upon their reasonable expectations.

With puberty, however, this seemingly straightforward progress from small to large, from ignorance to omniscience, from powerlessness to omnipotence, is disturbed. Motor controls have to be re-learned to deal with unexpected changes in physical size and structure; new emotions suddenly intrude upon the child, often at the most inconvenient and embarrassing moments; anxieties and fears which were thought to have been brought under control long since, unaccountably return with stronger force than ever. From the seemingly unassailable bastion of confidence from which the ten-year-old boy regards his world, a few short years has brought the adolescent to an insecure perch in his, exposed to anxieties, doubts and embarrassments he would not earlier have imagined possible.

We do not wish to exaggerate the young adolescent's unease, nor to pretend that the age does not have its rewards and compensations. The point to be insisted upon here is that with the onset of puberty comes a sense of uncertainty and consequent emotional insecurity which is something new in the child's experience. It is associated with, and is itself a powerful motive behind, a looking away from the family for a reference group[1]

[1] The term *reference group* is used by sociologists to denote a recognizable group of people whom the individual accepts as setting values and standards against which he measures his own behaviour and ideals. He need not, of course, necessarily be a member of his reference group—hence the technical distinction between an individual's membership groups (i.e., those social groups of which he is a member) and his reference groups.

which will provide a new pattern of behaviour and an alternative source of ideals, from which the adolescent can begin the long process, never entirely completed, of psychological weaning. In our Western European society, that reference group is normally found by young adolescents in informal groups of their own age; i.e., of their peers. The adolescent's peer-group[1] often governs his or her speech, dress, behaviour and attitudes with a degree of inflexibility that is the despair of parents. In return for the almost total conformity which the peer-group exacts of its members, it offers a source of emotional security from within which the adolescent may safely proceed along that path of parental and adult defiance which is essential to the full development of his personality.

We may see, then, that the peer-group is a natural form of social organization for the secondary schoolchild, and one in which powerful emotional mechanisms are already at work. The advantages of organizing groups on the basis of existing emotional attachments hardly needs emphasizing; it was certainly well known to the Greeks. Phaedrus, in his speech extolling love in Plato's *Symposium*, observes:

> If then one could contrive that a state or an army should entirely exist of lovers and loved, it would be impossible for it to have a better organization than that which it would then enjoy through their avoidance of all dishonour and their mutual emulation; moreover, a handful of such men, fighting side by side, would defeat practically the whole world.[2]

And, indeed, the famous *Sacred Band* of Thebes was said to be organized on such a principle.

In using group-work methods, then, the secondary school

[1] We have preferred the term *peer-group* to that of *gang*, which has too limited and pejorative a connotation and is anyway suggestive of a greater degree of organization and stability than the informal peer-group usually possesses. For a detailed study of the extent to which adolescents accept their peer-groups as reference groups, see Sherif & Sherif (1964), whose findings are confirmed in the recent study of adolescent boys in East London by Willmott (1966).

[2] Plato (1951), p. 43.

teacher is seeking to canalize a strongly felt drive which already exists in his pupils. That the underlying motive for associating in groups may derive primarily from their need to defy the adult world need not worry him unduly, for the greater security offered by such groups, and the greater consequent possibility of defiance, will be more than compensated for by the fact that the teacher at the same time as he forms the groups also removes himself from the role of obvious target. Indeed, the only signs of anti-adulthood that he might be able to detect in his own class-room may well be that sense of being excluded from the busy *camaraderie* of the groups themselves, his probable slight envy of which has already been mentioned.

That group work is psychologically appropriate to the teaching of adolescents is, of course, a generalization subject to particular qualifications. As Tanner has demonstrated,[1] not only is there an age difference of about two years between the onset of puberty in girls and that in boys, but also the age-range for any single such index with regard to either sex is very large indeed. For example, if we take the beginning of menstruation as an index which, while confined to girls, has the advantage of being clearly measurable, we find that the mean age of menarche among girls in Britain in 1960 was 13·1 years, with a normal range from 10 to 16 years.[2] That is, for some girls first to menstruate as early as ten while others do not begin until as late as sixteen is to be expected as part of a normal pattern, and there are exceptions outside even this wide range.

What we are saying is, of course, a matter of common know-ledge to every secondary teacher: that puberty covers an enor-mous age-range, and that in the same class one expects to find children demonstrating all stages of development, from those in whom the physiology of puberty has hardly manifested itself, to those who are physically mature. If, then, we accept that the psychological characteristics of puberty are particularly appro-priate to group work, we must qualify that fact with the recogni-tion that, in any secondary school class (not even excepting the

[1] Tanner (1961).
[2] *Ibid.*, p. 33.

sixth form in a boys' school), the maturational range will be considerable.

A second and equally important proviso is, of course, this: the statement that young adolescents draw emotional strength from the membership of peer-groups is a statement about a general tendency only; individuals may well not conform to this pattern, particularly those children who, on account of either an over-indulgent or an over-severe parent, are unable to deal with the intense anxiety or guilt which the process of psychological weaning will in their case give rise to.

A third objection that may be raised to the assertion that the psychology of adolescence is particularly well-suited to the use of group work, derives its force from the contradictory nature of adolescence itself. Anna Freud puts this tellingly:

Adolescents are excessively egoistic, regarding themselves as the centre of the universe and the sole object of interest, and yet at no time in later life are they capable of so much self-sacrifice and devotion. They form the most passionate love-relations, only to break them off as abruptly as they began them. On the one hand they throw themselves enthusiastically into the life of the community and, on the other, they have an overpowering longing for solitude. They oscillate between blind submission to some self-chosen leader and defiant rebellion against any and every authority. They are selfish and materially minded and at the same time full of lofty idealism. They are ascetic but will suddenly plunge into instinctual indulgence of the most primitive character. At times their behaviour to other people is rough and inconsiderate, yet they themselves are extremely touchy. Their moods vary between light-hearted optimism and the blackest pessimism. Sometimes they will work with indefatigable enthusiasm and at other times they are sluggish and apathetic.[1]

Even allowing for the deliberate antithesis of this vivid description, one cannot help feeling at first sight that the personality so described is hardly likely to make the most effective, nor yet the most welcome, contribution to a co-operative venture. And yet we would maintain that group work in fact provides the best available method for absorbing these contradictory modes of

[1] Freud (1937), pp. 149-50.

behaviour, simply because the work is child-directed and as a result each member is able, within reason, to adjust his contribution to suit his mood. When the teacher has laid down not only the work to be done, but also the manner in which it is to be done, the conditions under which it is to be done, and the time by which it has to be done, then the pupil who wishes to vary the circumstances to suit his mood can only accept the consequences of disobeying the teacher's instructions. With group work, however, the work proceeds under the direction of the children themselves. This provides not only for variation in the nature and extent of each individual's contribution, but also for that individual to vary the rate at which his contribution proceeds. Of course, if all the members of the group are coincidentally in a 'sluggish and apathetic' mood, then the work will obviously slow down, and if, during discussion, 'their behaviour to other people is rough and inconsiderate' or 'they have an overpowering longing for solitude', it is unlikely that they will arrive at a wise decision. But it will nevertheless be seen on reflection that the group-work approach does offer the moody child an opportunity to adjust to the work without the constant threat of punishment if he fails to conform to a predetermined pattern of working.

THE PSYCHOLOGY OF MENTAL DEVELOPMENT

Reference has already been made to the work of the Swiss psychologist, Jean Piaget. Piaget has shown that the growing child's comprehension of the world about him depends very largely upon the richness and variety of his sensory experiences, and that his capacity for forming concepts about the world grows out of these experiences. The majority of children are not capable of understanding abstract concepts until adolescence, and what many teachers have taken for understanding has in fact been elaborate chains of learned responses, having little or no meaning for the child who has learnt them. The ability to undertake what Piaget terms *formal operations*—that is, to be able logically to manipulate propositions independent of their relation to the concrete world about him; to form hypotheses and test them in imagination; systematically to work through all possible explanations of an abstract problem—this ability is not normally found in children before the age of fourteen or fifteen; indeed, with limited endowment and an unfavourable environment, it may never develop at all.

Piaget's findings have already contributed to the change in primary school method which has been spreading slowly but surely throughout the English educational system. Their impact on secondary schools, however, has been much slower, though they are just as relevant. Piaget has shown that while eleven- and twelve-year old children are normally capable of understanding logical relationships, they must still be based largely upon tangible experience. It is precisely this kind of experience that group work is designed to provide. In working through formal mathematical exercises, the first- or second-year secondary-school child is applying a series of learned responses, with greater or less success according to his capacity for rote learning and his experience of rewards and punishments. These calculations constitute a closed system, having virtually no relation to the world outside the classroom and exercise book. In using graphs or diagrams to illustrate the findings of an investigation, however, the child is starting from the open system of his own experience. Because the facts which he is concerned to illustrate have meaning for him, because they are based on the evidence of his own senses, he will not use mathematical procedures to present them unless or until he can manipulate those procedures with confidence. And because he can always test them against the known basis of his own discoveries, he will not be tempted to substitute the mere rote learning of those procedures for their proper understanding.

From this point of view it might be argued that while a case can be made out for using group work in the junior forms of secondary schools, where the majority of children are still at that stage in the development of their logical thinking called by Piaget the stage of *concrete operations*, it would seem to be inappropriate as a method for older children, many of whom can handle abstract concepts without recourse to their tangible or visual representation. Here, however, a further point made by Piaget bears consideration. In the concluding chapter of his book, *The Growth of Logical Thinking from Childhood to Adolescence*, he draws attention to the adolescent's need to express his dissatisfaction with the adult world about him, and in some way to work through the measures with which he would reform it—with which, indeed he *intends* to reform it. Piaget points out that this is an essential factor in the process of achieving autonomy and hence adult responsibility.

As opposed to the child who feels inferior and subordinate to the adult, the adolescent is an individual who begins to consider himself as the equal of adults and to judge them, with complete reciprocity, on the same plane as himself. But to this first trait, two others are indissolubly related. The adolescent is an individual who is still growing, but one who begins to think of the future—i.e., of his present or future work in society. Thus, to his current activities he adds a life program for later 'adult' activities. Further, in most cases in our societies, the adolescent is the individual who in attempting to plan his present or future work in adult society also has the idea (from his point of view, it is directly related to his plans) of changing this society, whether in some limited area or completely. Thus it is impossible to fill an adult role without conflicts, and whereas the child looks for resolution of his conflicts in present-day compensations (real or imaginary), the adolescent adds to these limited compensations the more general compensation of a motivation for change, or even specific planning for change.[1]

We have already seen this process at work in the investigation into the occupational structure of the neighbourhood undertaken by a fifth-year examination class under the guidance of their teacher. It was precisely this opportunity to test their views of the adult society which they were themselves upon the brink of entering that the group work afforded, and afforded in a more purposeful and realistic setting than any formal classroom activity could have done.

Group work, then, can be shown not only to offer the opportunities for the kind of sensory experience which Piaget and his

---

[1] Inhelder & Piaget (1958), pp. 338-9.

followers have demonstrated is still necessary to the majority of children in the lower forms of secondary schools, but also to provide an acceptable framework within which the older adolescent can work out, realistically and meaningfully, his own changing role as he approaches adulthood.

DISCIPLINE VERSUS SELF-DIRECTION

We have spoken earlier of the flexibility which group work provides, and which allows children to work at their own pace. This very flexibility may be seen by some as an argument against it. The view is often advanced that children have to learn to adjust themselves when they grow up to a world in which there is little or no provision for temperamental differences, and that if we allow them to suit themselves in the pace with which they apply themselves to their school work, they will become lazy and finical, unfitted to do an honest day's work.

This view represents one side of a basic and continuing controversy which is to be found wherever there are teachers and others concerned with the upbringing of children. This controversy is between those who take the view that a child's nature is basically selfish and potentially tyrannical, and that the educator's task is that of teaching self-control through the experience of the discipline imposed by elders and betters (we may call this the *disciplinarian viewpoint*), and those who take the view that while a child's nature is no doubt basically self-interested, it is potentially co-operative, and that the educator's task is that of teaching self-control through the experience of the rewards of shared pleasures and purposes (we may call this the *self-rewarding viewpoint*).

The classic spokesman in this country for the disciplinarian point of view is John Locke:

It seems plain to me, that the Principle of all Virtue and Excellency lies in a Power of denying our selves the satisfaction of our own Desires, where Reason does not authorize them. This Power is to be got and improved by Custom, made easy and familiar by an early Practice. If therefore I might be heard, I

GWSS—D

would advise that, contrary to the ordinary Way, children should be us'd to submit their Desires, and go without their Longings, even *from their very Cradles*. The first Thing they should learn to know, should be, that they were not to have any Thing because it pleased them, but because it was thought fit for them. . . .

He that has not a Mastery over his Inclinations, he that knows not how to resist the Importunity of *present Pleasure or Pain*, for the sake of what Reason tells him is fit to be done, wants the true Principle of Virtue and Industry, and is in danger never to be good for anything. This Temper, therefore, so contrary to unguided Nature, is to be got betimes; and this Habit, as the true Foundation of future Ability and Happiness, is to be wrought into the Mind as early as may be, even from the first Dawnings of Knowledge or Apprehension in Children, and so to be confirm'd in them, by all the Care and Ways imaginable, by those who have the Oversight of their Education.[1]

The basic assumption of the disciplinarian is that the child does not have the capacity for self-direction, even within a general framework of order, and that consequently he has to be instructed carefully with regard to the whole range of behaviour which the adult wishes to influence (which is virtually all his behaviour since even in play children are expected to conform for the most part to adult expectations), and then supervised regularly until the desired mode of action has become habitual through repetition, the need for adult approval and the fear of punishment.

It does not much matter whether this view of child nature proceeds from supernatural convictions, such as the Christian belief that all children are born in original sin, or from such quasi-scientific theories as those of Rudolf Steiner who sees children as 'needing' authoritarian direction from adults until they have reached the age of fourteen,[2] or from generalizations based upon the observation of how children in fact do behave—the outcome is the same and is to be seen in any classroom or home, and to be heard justified in any staffroom or supermarket.

The belief in the effectiveness of imposed discipline in its most optimistic form is that to be found in that school prize so beloved by all disciplinarians: *Tom Brown's Schooldays.*

[1] Locke (1884) pp. 25 and 29.
[2] See Steiner (1954).

Five minutes afterwards the master of their form, a late arrival and a model young master, knocks at the Doctor's study door. 'Come in!' and as he enters the Doctor goes on, to Holmes, [a sixth-former and house-prefect] 'You see, I do not know anything of the case officially; and if I take any notice of it at all, I must publicly expel the boy. I don't wish to do that, for I think there is some good in him. There's nothing for it but a good sound thrashing.' He paused to shake hands with the master, which Holmes does also, and then prepares to leave.

'I understand. Good-night, sir.'

'Good-night, Holmes. And remember,' added the Doctor, emphasizing the words, 'a good sound thrashing before the whole house.'

The door closed on Holmes; and the Doctor, in answer to the puzzled look of his lieutenant, explained shortly. 'A gross case of bullying. Wharton, the head of the house, is a very good fellow, but slight and weak, and severe physical pain is the only way to deal with such a case; so I have asked Holmes to take it up. He is very careful and trustworthy, and has plenty of strength. I wish all the sixth had as much. We must have it here, if we are to keep order at all.'

Now I don't want any wiseacres to read this book; but if they should, of course they will prick up their long ears, and howl, or rather bray, at the above story. Very good, I don't object; but what I have to add for you boys is this, that Holmes called a levy of his house after breakfast next morning, made them a speech on the case of the bullying in question, and then gave the bully a 'good sound thrashing'; and that years afterwards, that boy sought out Holmes, and thanked him, saying it had been the kindest act which had ever been done upon him, and the turning-point in his character; and a very good fellow he became, and a credit to his school.[1]

With the disciplinarians we may place Plato, the Jesuits, the sadistic Dr. Keate of Eton, Truby King (a man who has probably been responsible for more misery in the world than almost any other), that whole gallery of child-beaters depicted by Dickens, and, indeed, most of the teaching profession throughout the nineteenth century and, we dare say, throughout a good deal of the twentieth. We do not have to look back into history to find teachers who rely on the rod, even if such public floggings as that

[1] Hughes (n.d.) pp. 212-13.

described by George Lamming in his autobiographical novel, *In the Castle of My Skin*,[1] are becoming unusual in this country; although we may note in passing that even the recommendations of the Plowden Committee that corporal punishment should be abolished in *primary* schools[2] (which itself was not a unanimous recommendation) led to protests in the press from a representative body of headmasters and headmistresses.

But it is not, of course, upon what Tom Brown's headmaster called 'a good sound thrashing' that the case of the disciplinarians rests, and we may find many who, convinced of the need for imposed discipline, strongly oppose recourse to physical violence, or at any rate to the kind of severity which the Doctor recommended. As Locke himself said:

Severity carry'd to the highest Pitch . . . often brings in the room of it . . . a *low spirited moap'd Creature*, who, however with his unnatural Sobriety he may please silly People, who commend tame unactive Children, because they make no Noise, nor give them any Trouble; yet at last, will probably prove as uncomfortable a Thing to his Friends, as he will be all his Life a useless Thing to himself and others.[3]

Nevertheless, the control which Locke and others would use to 'submit the appetites to reason' is an aversive one, and is firmly based upon the negative formulation of the Law of Effect: that all organisms (including children) seek to avoid repeating behaviour which in the past has brought them pain. To quote Skinner:

The child at his desk, filling in his workbook, is behaving primarily to escape from the threat of a series of minor aversive events—the teacher's displeasure, the criticism or ridicule of his classmates, an ignominious showing in a competition, low marks, a trip to the office 'to be talked to' by the principal, or a word to the parent who may still resort to the birch rod.[4]

---

[1] Lamming (1953).
[2] Education & Science, Dept. of (1967), vol. i, p. 272.
[3] Locke (1884), p. 31.
[4] Skinner (1960), p. 104.

The disciplinarian argument, therefore, rests upon the validity of aversive controls as a means of socializing the child, and while there might not be many today who would see in a public flogging a control suitable for general application (though there are more than the reader of this book may suppose), the essential core of the argument—that education must proceed by dissuasion—remains.

To this we have opposed the 'self-rewarding' argument, which starts from the assumption that a positive approach to socialization is both more effective and also to be preferred on humanitarian grounds. In fact, of course, the core of this viewpoint—that education should proceed by persuasion—is equally firmly based upon the Law of Effect, only upon its positive form: that all organisms (including children) seek to repeat behaviour which in the past has brought them pleasure, or the satisfaction of a need. As children grow older, they find increasingly that such pleasure is to be had in each other's company, in joint pursuits. Whether or not we posit the existence of an 'instinct' of gregariousness, we can start from the observation that the vast majority of older children enjoy the company of their coevals, particularly if in addition they enjoy their approval. The seeking of this enjoyment may itself constitute a very powerful motive for action, and if it can be linked with an activity which is valued for its own sake, and the two factors related to some educational purpose, a positive condition of learning is found of far greater potential than all but the most dreaded punishments. This is, of course, the situation that the teacher using group work hopes to attain. The techniques and knowledge gained in a successful group-work undertaking, since they have been attended by the double pleasure of preferred company and selected activity, will be thus doubly reinforced; that is to say, their recall and repetition on future occasions is made highly likely.

But there is a further reinforcement inherent in the situation. The greater the individual's contribution to the common task, the greater will be his fellow-members' approval of him (always assuming, of course, he does not seek to usurp their own functions, or try to dominate them). For this reason he will strive to improve his own part in the work, thus earning more approval. But a greater mastery of his own skills, or a wider grasp of that area of knowledge for which he is responsible, will in turn bring its own reward: that deriving from his satisfaction and pride in his new achievements. There is thus created a condition of a positive feedback, which can lead, through acceleration, to results which will astonish both the teacher and the child himself. (It is the same mechanism which enabled the Stakhanovite workers to claim production increases of up to tenfold).

THE LIPPITT AND WHITE EXPERIMENTS

The argument in favour of group work as an effective aid to learning does not rest upon theoretical considerations alone. There is now a good deal of supporting evidence from the experiments of social psychologists.[1] Of these experiments, those of Lippitt and White, already referred to, are the most famous; indeed, they must be the most often quoted experiments in the whole field of social psychology. Until recently it has not been easy for the teacher without access to a research library to read the original reports.[2] However, in 1960 the authors published *Autocracy and Democracy*,[3] which contains a full description of the experiments.

Briefly, the major series of experiments consisted of observing and recording very carefully the behaviour of four 'clubs' of eleven-year-old boys. Each club consisted of a group of five boys who met in their spare time under an adult leader to engage in various hobbies and pursuits. Each club had three series of meetings under three different leaders. The role fulfilled by the leader, and his expressed attitude towards the boys and their activities, constituted the main variable of the experiment, and every effort was made to ensure that all other variables, such as those of the boys' social adjustment, their sociometric status, their social and

---

[1] Much of the relevant evidence was summarized in Fleming (1951). More recent summaries are to be found in the volumes edited by Berkowitz (1964), by Hare (1962) and by Hare and others (1965).

[2] Lewin, Lippitt & White (1939), Lippitt (1940).

[3] White & Lippitt (1960).

educational background, and so forth, were held constant by matching, or neutralized by random variation. Three main roles were defined: they were those of the autocratic leader, the *laissez-faire* leader and the democratic leader, and the behaviour and attitudes appropriate to each role were clearly laid down. The autocratic leader was to initiate all policies and direct all the club activities, step by step. He was not to explain the overall plan beforehand, so that each member of the club would be entirely reliant on him for instructions at each stage of the work. He was to dictate what the club activity should be, and to allocate individual tasks. Where a task needed more than one worker, he was to decide who should work with whom. His praise and blame was to be expressed in personal terms, implying thereby approval or disapproval of the individual child. He was not to participate in the work except by way of giving a demonstration how something should be done.

The *laissez-faire* leader was to allow members of the group complete freedom in deciding on what was to be done and how to do it, whether this was done by discussion or by individual decisions. He was to supply such materials as were needed, and to answer questions only when asked. He was not to participate at any stage of the work. He could make occasional spontaneous comments, but he was not to attempt any appraisal of the activities either of the group as a whole, or of individual members.

The democratic leader was to get the group to formulate policy through discussion and agreement, in which his own role was that of encouraging and assisting. He was to make sure that all members of the group saw the overall plan. He was to give alternative suggestions for work methods, but to encourage the group to accept responsibility for final choice. He was to allow the members of the group to choose work-mates, and to divide the tasks among themselves. His comments were to be objective and confined to an appraisal of the work itself; he was to avoid personal praise or blame.

In order to ensure that the personality of the adults fulfilling these roles did not bias the results, each adult fulfilled at least two of the roles with different clubs, and the experimental design provided for clubs to experience the different adults and roles in varying sequences, thus attempting to control the variables inherent in the experiment itself. In addition to the 'normal' situation of the club meeting under a leader, special test situations were devised. These were those of the leader arriving late; of his being called out; of the arrival, during the leader's absence, of an outsider who then criticized the club's activities; and of the presence of a group of children from another school.

A number of activities were pursued by the clubs, including woodwork, painting, decorating, making masks, taking casts of footprints, soap-carving, model-aeroplane construction, and so forth.

The Lippitt and White experiments are justifiably famous, not only for their experimental ingenuity, but also for the care which was taken to make the observations (undertaken by a team of research assistants), both objective and rigorous. Thus two observers made a stenographic record of all that was said; another observer recorded social interactions in terms of predetermined categories; another kept a minute-by-minute record of the subgroup structures that were formed; yet another recorded intergroup reactions. The club leaders wrote up their own accounts after each session, and interviews were held with the children at the end of each series of meetings. Interviews were also held with their parents, and there were many other cross-checks. This altogether admirable methodological rigour did have the result, however, that it is difficult to summarize the data without also thereby interpreting them. We think that a careful examination of the reports would confirm the following, admittedly interpretative, conclusions.

Under an autocratic leader, children work reasonably industriously provided the leader is present, though if he is absent the work immediately slackens off, and horseplay and other forms of tension-release frequently occur. While the work done while the leader is present is usually carefully executed, the children show little initiative in dealing with even small problems, relying upon the leader for instruction. They also appear to be dependent upon his approval for any satisfaction, and such self-criticism as they show is not based on objective standards. A good deal of personal frustration appears to be engendered by the authoritarian 'social climate'; whether or not this is expressed as aggressive behaviour seems to depend upon the actual personality of the leader and/or of the children. In the experiments, two kinds of reactions to autocracy were manifested: in the aggressive reaction, the children showed a high degree of hostility towards each other (as measured by aggressive remarks and behaviour), though this decreased dramatically with the appearance of an outsider who acted as a scapegoat—for example the critical janitor (in reality, of course, a research assistant). In the submissive reaction to autocracy, the general incidence of hostility between the members of the group was very much less, though there was still a good deal of hostility displayed towards the outsider. Both forms of reaction to authoritarianism involved low scores for friendliness to either the leader or to the other children, and little evidence of pleasure being derived from what was, after all, a voluntary pastime. When the club activity was the making of papier-mâché masks, for instance, the autocratically led club celebrated the final meeting by destroying with a good deal of violence the mask they had laboriously made.

Under a *laissez-faire* leader, children worked spasmodically and even appeared to do more work when he was absent than when he was present. Application to the task in hand was frequently interrupted by disorganized and apparently aimless play, and there was a certain amount of pure loafing—a form of behaviour almost entirely absent from the other social climates. When the *laissez-faire* club had finished their mask, they left it in the clubroom, no one seeming to want to bother with it.

Under a democratic leader, children worked regularly, though not as well in terms of pure industry as under an autocratic leader. However, the level of work was hardly affected by whether or not the leader was present, nor were they particularly upset by his arriving late. Conversation was more work-minded than in even the authoritarian-submissive reaction, and a high percentage of the children's remarks consisted of suggestions relevant to the

92 *The rationale of group work*

task. Democratically led children displayed the highest amount of friendly behaviour to each other and to the leader. Whereas in both the authoritarian and *laissez-faire* social climates there was a certain amount of deliberate ignoring of the leader's remarks, there was a negligible amount of this in the democratic climate, and a much higher proportion of remarks included the leader in referring to the total group.

Perhaps the most revealing data from these experiments are those which record attitudes to work during the absence of the leader. As has been stated above, one of the experimental variables was the calling-out of the leader during a session, and his re-appearance some time later. The different reactions to this situation by the four types of social climate (allowing for two kinds of reaction to authoritarianism) are marked. One of the categories of observation was the percentage of each child's time spent in 'high-activity involvement' with the work. The following table gives the relevant data: [1]

Percentage of the time spent by the children in 'high-activity involvement' in the work when:

Reactions	(a) the leader is in	(b) the leader is out	(c) the leader has just returned
Autocratic-Aggressive	52%	17%	58%
Autocratic-Submissive	74%	29%	81%
Laissez-Faire	31%	49%	19%
Democratic	49%	47%	39%

The implications of these figures are inescapable. If we regard as the main aim of teaching the conditioning of children to work well so long as they are supervised, but to slack immediately the supervisor leaves, then it would appear that we should submit them to authoritarian teachers. If, in addition, these teachers are so severe, and the children so terrified of them, that they are unable to manifest the hostility which their servitude engenders,

[1] Constructed from data given in Lippitt & White (1958), p. 503, fig. 3.

unless it be to some unfortunate scapegoat, then we may count on a high level of unimaginative work during, but for no longer than, the period of their instruction. If, on the other hand, we would not consider their capacity for working as of much relevance to their schooling, and if we would have them become giddy-heads, unable to apply themselves for any period of time to one thing, least of all when an adult is at hand, then we must appoint as teachers men with a capacity for doing nothing, and with no real interest in children or their activities. But if our concern in submitting our children to organized education is to make them capable of sustained and thoughtful work, regardless of whether or not they are under supervision, and if we want them to be able to look at their own work self-critically, to accept the valid criticisms of others without resentment, and above all, to find in a common task a source of enjoyment and satisfaction, it seems that we would be well advised to appoint to our schools neither strict disciplinarians, nor uninterested clock-watchers, however easy-going, but men practised in the skills of group democracy, sufficiently interested in them to be able to offer advice and help when asked. In other words, we should appoint good group-work teachers.

We have discussed the Lippitt and White experiments at some length not only because of their obvious relevance to group work, but also because, although they are now over a quarter of a century old, their basic findings still hold. However, it would be wrong to leave them without some reference to more recent work in this field. On the whole, subsequent experiments have confirmed Lippitt and White's main conclusions that children work more harmoniously, and with a higher standard as far as qualitative output is concerned, in a democratic atmosphere, while more sheer quantity of work may be produced under an authoritarian regime, provided the authority is continually present. The work of Bavelas[1] and of Anderson and Brewer[2] is reported in Richardson's summary;[3] their studies of playground leadership and of

[1] Bavelas (1942).
[2] Anderson & Brewer (1945-6).
[3] Richardson (1951).

classroom behaviour, tended to support Lippitt and White's findings in particular details as well as in general. More recent work, however, has shown that the superiority of a democratic approach is not necessarily applicable to adult learning situations (in which workers may well have particular expectations about how a foreman or other leader should behave), and that small groups in which there are two or more strongly assertive leaders may well fail to work satisfactorily. To be fair, this last discovery is one that was anticipated by Lippitt and White themselves, and recent work in the whole field of small group psychology has concerned itself much more with the changing nature of relationships within the group than with the relationship of the whole group to outside authority.[1]

THE DEUTSCH EXPERIMENTS

The experiments of Lippitt and White do not constitute the only experimental evidence in favour of group-work methods from the point of view of developing desirable attitudes towards work, though they are probably the most suggestive from our point of view in their contrast between the authoritarian and democratic roles played by the adults. Another experiment, this time with students, is that carried out by Morton Deutsch.[2] He created two kinds of classroom attitudes in relation to a course on psychology: co-operative and competitive. The course for all classes was organized into discussion groups, which met to analyse and discuss problems and case histories. The members of some classes were told their grades for the course would be based on the general quality of these discussions, and that each member of a class would receive the group mark, while the members of other classes were told their grades depended upon their own individual contributions, and that they would be ranked in order from best to worst according to the quality of each member's comments. Thus the members of the co-operative classes de-

---

[1] A good summary of recent work in the social psychology of leadership is that of Fiedler in Berkowitz (1964) volume 1, pp. 149-90.
[2] Deutsch (1949).

pended for good marks upon the whole class contributing well to the discussion, while the members of the competitive classes depended for good marks on being able to outshine the other members.

The results of this experiment were most striking. Although the two sets of classes were selected at random, and were dealing with identical material, they behaved in quite different ways. The members of the co-operative groups were able to communicate with each other more effectively than those in the competitive groups; they took more account of the contributions of others in their own comments; they were more friendly towards each other; and they were much more satisfied with the group's performance than were the members of the competitive groups. Deutsch was also able to show that whereas in the co-operative groups a good deal of energy was devoted to making it easy for each member to make his contribution, and that members' contributions were integrated into the general discussion by other members, in the competitive groups individuals devoted their energies to trying to dominate and outshine their fellows. But the most interesting outcome of the experiment was the fact that the co-operative groups produced more ideas in each discussion than did the competitive groups, and that furthermore, the quality of the ideas produced was better.

This last finding is one that may well be brought into question by those who attach prime importance to the value of competition as an incentive to learning, and we must remember that Deutsch's experiment was with college students not schoolchildren, and that it was concerned with the contributions of ideas to discussions, not the giving of answers to predetermined questions. Nevertheless, it seems probable that his findings are applicable to older children. Certainly it is the common experience of those teachers who have applied group-work methods that energies that ordinarily go into trying to outshine and dominate other children may well instead be devoted to co-operative enterprises, and that often those children who are most aggressive and domineering in a competitive situation prove to be those who are most helpful to their fellows in a co-operative one. Moreover, we have already given psychological reasons for thinking that adolescents gain particular emotional satisfaction from working on a task with others of their own age, in so far as a shared purpose provides that sense of security which the adolescent needs to allow him to identify with his peer-group.

However, there is one consideration arising out of Deutsch's last finding which ought to be mentioned here, and that is the encouragement of individual enterprise. Without bringing into question the validity of Deutsch's finding—that ideas produced in a co-operative group are superior in quality to those produced in a competitive group—it may well be objected that an education which encourages children to give of their best only in co-operation with their fellows may well be limiting, particularly in a society based upon individual enterprise. Moreover, it can be argued that even the best ideas produced in a co-operative situation are likely to be conformist; in other words, that such a situation is not likely to encourage the really revolutionary thinker, though it can be shown that many of our cultural and technological advances were initiated by individuals who had such a capacity for revolutionary thinking. These are fundamental questions involving the consideration of the basic aims of education, a full discussion of which would be out of place here. We may say, however, that much as we may think it desirable to encourage original thinking in our children, by far the major part of their secondary education, at least before they reach the sixth form, must necessarily be the learning and application of orthodox ideas, and if Deutsch's finding are relevant to secondary schooling—and we think they probably are—then it would appear that such learning is likely to be more effective in a co-operative situation.

OTHER EXPERIMENTAL EVIDENCE

So far we have been concerned with experimental evidence to support the argument that democratic and co-operative groups are more conducive to effective learning than authoritarian and competitive ones. There is also a good deal of evidence to demonstrate that children are more ready to accept the authority of their own fellows than that of the teacher—a finding that most teachers are understandably reluctant to accept! In a study published in 1950,[1] Ruth Berenda, repeating Solomon Asch's well-known experiments, showed that children were prepared to accept the authority of their classmates even to the extent of distrusting their own senses and agreeing with what they could see to be incorrect judgements—for example, in comparing the lengths of lines on the blackboard—but they could not be so persuaded by their teachers. Moreover, while the majority of the children were ready to change their own opinions in order to fall in line with what they took to be the views of their group, they were strongly resistant to the influence of the teacher, and it was only the younger children who were prepared to doubt their own senses on the teacher's authority. While we may well regret that children (like many adults) prefer to trust the judgement of their fellows to the evidence of their own senses, we may also draw the inference that learning which is reinforced by the experience of the whole group is likely to be more efficient than that which proceeds solely from the authority of the teacher.

Relevant here is that branch of social psychology of recent but extremely rapid growth concerned with what are known as T-groups. The T is short for *training*, and training groups are groups expressly formed to enable their members to learn the mechanisms of group dynamics through the observation and analysis of their own group proceedings. Through becoming aware of their own often irrational and unconsciously motivated behaviour in T-group sessions, their members learn the importance of personal factors in all human relationships, particularly where those relationships ostensibly are concerned with other areas—for example, the organization of work in a factory. While the term T-group originated in the United States, and is particularly associated with the work of the National Training Laboratory in Group Development at Bethel, Maine and elsewhere, similar approaches were being made in Britain, particularly at the Tavistock Institute in London, and at the University of

[1] Berenda (1950).

Leicester.[1] T-group theory has so far been almost wholly concerned with the experiences of adults in group-learning situations; indeed, a recent summary of the literature is sub-titled 'Innovation in Re-education' and the emphasis in many studies is upon the need to re-learn many of our basic assumptions about human behaviour. However, it is almost certain that this latest branch of social psychology will come to concern itself with the intra-group dynamics of children's and adolescents' groups. When it does, it seems highly likely that one of the basic findings will be equally relevant—that is, the need in any task-related group to provide an opportunity for members to work through to a commitment to the common task in accordance with their own emotional needs, and it is, of course, this need that is met in group work by the necessary provision of discussion and free choice.

One worker in this field who deserves special mention here is Thelen, who is one of the few social psychologists who has attempted not only to show the relevance of small group theory to teaching, but also to make concrete suggestions as to how that relevance can be built upon.[2] Thelen's recommendations are very much in line with what we are describing in the present volume. And no book on the subject of group work, however brief, can afford to ignore the pioneering work of Oeser and his associates, who mounted the first large-scale attempt to train teachers in discussion group methods outside the United States.[3]

Finally, there is a large amount of experimental evidence to show that with children, as with adults, the springs of action depend upon the needs of individuals, among the most important of which is the need for social recognition and approval. One of the most illuminating contributions made by social psychology to

---

[1] A good recent summary of American work is that edited by Bradford and others (1964). One of the Tavistock Institute's most entertaining, as well as provocative writers, is Bion (1961). A classical study of the application of the technique to factory organization is that of Jaques (1951), while a recent approach to training based on a learning group is that of Ottaway (1966). Finally, Mills (1964) has demonstrated the life cycle of one such group.

[2] See Thelen (1954), particularly chapters 2 and 3.

[3] Oeser (1960).

man's understanding of himself stems from the discovery of the fact that a good deal of his so-called economic behaviour is motivated, not by his need to maximize material wealth, as is assumed by the economic textbooks, but by his need for social recognition and approval. The classic Hawthorne experiments in the nineteen-twenties and early thirties showed that factory workers responded to variations in their break times and canteen arrangements with increased production, no matter what the variations were. It was demonstrated that it was a response to the interest shown in them by the management and research workers that led to the increase rather than any material advantage obtained from the different arrangements.[1] Since then a large number of studies have shown the importance of social recognition as a spur to human endeavour whether in the factory, office or classroom. Peer-groups provide opportunities for the satisfaction of this basic need, and peer-groups with a common purpose— as in the case of group work—afford many such opportunities. Learning which is associated with need-satisfaction of this order is doubly reinforced, because the work itself is the occasion of the social recognition.

Group work, then, can be shown to have powerful psychological arguments in its favour, both from the point of view of the special problems of the adolescent, and from the general findings of social psychology. In a successful group-work undertaking, the pupils taking part form a peer-group of the kind that supports the long process of psychological weaning. The fact that it has a common and agreed purpose gives the group the kind of authority that the older child needs and seeks, without attaching that authority directly to a teacher. In this way group work avoids the pattern of behaviour, well known by teachers in the middle school, in which the thirteen- and fourteen-year-old rejects school work as part of his overall defiance of the adult world. Because the group task is chosen by the children themselves, and because they have responsibility for its planning and direction, the work no longer represents a chore imposed by adult authority, but becomes a symbol of their own emancipation. This

[1] Mayo (1949)

is one of the reasons why the teacher's part in the work should
be as unobtrusive as possible. At the same time, and true to the
paradoxical logic of adolescence, the very fact that the teacher is
there as an ultimate authority provides the adult recognition that
the adolescent needs while he is trying to establish his inde-
pendence.

But as we have shown, membership of a purposeful (or goal-
directed) group satisfies needs that are not limited to the period
of adolescence. Social psychology has demonstrated that a craving
for social recognition and approval is one of the most potent
springs of action for most people, whether child or adult. The
peer-group provides an ideal nexus for the satisfaction of this
basic need.[1]

[1] Readers who wish to pursue further the contributions of social
psychology should consult the collection of papers in Maccoby *et al.*
(1958). A standard work on the psychology of groups is that of Cartwright and Zander (1960), while an application of social psychological
theories to the classroom will be found in Bany and Johnson (1964).

7 Training teachers in group-work methods

There are a number of difficulties to be overcome in training student-teachers in group-work methods, most of them stemming from their own school experience. As we have said, the majority of students in colleges and university departments of education come from grammar or public schools in which the tradition of teaching is almost universally that of formal, teacher-directed, class teaching. Moreover, the students themselves were usually among the brighter children; that is, they were normally in A-stream classes, occasionally in B-streams, and only very rarely in C-streams. Thus, not only was their own experience almost entirely that of formal teaching, but also it was of reasonably successful formal teaching and they themselves learnt reasonably successfully from it. Over their secondary-school years they mastered the techniques demanded by formal teaching and traditional examinations, and it is indeed to this mastery that they owe their entrance to college or university. Hence, when they finally begin their own training as teachers, those students who are going to teach in secondary schools expect to teach in the same way they were themselves taught.

This expectation governs their own attitude towards training. Starting from the view of the teacher as a source of knowledge whose task is somehow to instil this knowledge into his pupils, the students reasonably see their own purpose as primarily that of acquiring the necessary extra knowledge to make them authorities in their chosen subjects, together with the mastering of the methods of teaching those subjects. Moreover, they expect to learn both their subject background and also the method of teaching it in the same way. Student teachers are usually very conscious of the problems of classroom management, and this consciousness is heightened by their experience on teaching practice. But the solution to these problems is sought in terms of techniques which can be learned, rather than in terms of relationships between teacher and taught. While they will pay lip-service to the importance of understanding children's motivation in their education essays, they will at the same time continue to speak and behave as if effective teaching depends largely upon the application of a set of universal nostrums which can be written down and learnt in the same way that history notes were written down and learnt, and which it is their tutors' duty to provide. Indeed, the failure of tutors to do just this is often one of the main criticisms made by students of their professional course.

Thus the majority of students regard the idea of group work in secondary school with suspicion deriving from its unfamiliarity and from their own academic success under conventional teaching methods, and this suspicion is aggravated by their own anxieties about being face to face with a class. Faced on teaching practice for the first time with classes of older children who are apathetic or even openly hostile to learning, they seek urgently for a solution within the only framework they know—that is, the formal class-teaching lesson—and the more disorderly their own lessons become, the more desperately they cling to the idea of 'techniques' of class control. Hence, to the suspicion with which they regard group work is added an impatience with the time wasted, which should—in their view—be devoted to the vastly more urgent problems of mastering the techniques of teaching.

A further problem, which to some extent arises out of the same situation, is an understandable reluctance on the part of the student who has managed to achieve a somewhat precarious control over his classes with one approach to begin again with a totally different approach.

THE STUDENT'S NEED OF PRIOR SELF-CONFIDENCE IN A FORMAL TEACHING SITUATION

The student's own expectations regarding the teaching methods they are going to use relate, as we have said, almost exclusively to formal methods. And to be fair, the vast majority of schools to which they will be appointed (at the time of writing, at any rate) will expect them to teach formally. Thus, in the three-year college course with which we are ourselves concerned, we have felt it proper to postpone an introduction to group-work methods in a course of teacher training until the students have gained some confidence using formal methods. Hence, the first year of training is aimed at achieving competence in basic skills in the traditional teacher-directed lessons. Naturally, students are encouraged to plan for a high level of pupil-participation, with the children learning through personal discovery and experience, though within a framework determined in advance by the teacher. Lesson notes are expected to provide for both the more and the less able children in the class, and to give individual children the opportunity of using their own initiative. All this is quite possible within the traditional framework, given realistic and thoughtful preparation of lessons in relation to the known abilities and background of the children—and if the classes are small enough to allow the teacher time to deal with the children's individual needs.

By the end of the first year of training, most students have acquired a reasonable competence in a traditional classroom situation and several have already begun to see some of the limitations of formal teaching. By now they have sufficient self-confidence to be able to look back critically on their own schooling; they find that they have already forgotten most of what they swotted for O and A levels, and even in the subjects they are studying to a higher level in college they discover fundamental gaps in their understanding.

Thus the second year of the three-year course has seemed to us to be an appropriate time for the introduction of group work and other experimental methods.While the majority of students would probably prefer to have further experience in traditional classroom teaching, as we have said, yet they have reached a position of relative self-confidence which enables them to consider alternatives. The knowledge that if they are unable to deal with their classes in these new methods, they can revert to a formal situation which they have already found themselves able to handle, is an important factor in their willingness to consider them.

THE NEED FOR PERSONAL EXPERIENCE OF GROUP WORK

It is not only lack of self-confidence that presents a problem. The students themselves have often had no personal experience of group work, and even those who have worked in this way in their primary schools may well doubt whether the approach is suitable for older pupils. For this reason it is very desirable for students to be able to see group work in progress in secondary schools under the guidance of experienced teachers. From observing groups at work it is a very short step to working with the groups themselves—one student to a group of five to six children. Now the students are able not only to see for themselves the extent to which children become involved in what they are doing—they may even find themselves sharing this involvement.

An alternative, or better still a preliminary, to observing children doing group work is for the students themselves to undertake group topics with their tutors taking the role of group-work teachers. This is a valuable exercise for two reasons: one is that they discover for themselves the springs of action which lead to the kind of involvement with their work which may well have been outside their experience before this. Students who are the first to close their notebooks at the end of a lecture, whose essays are of minimum length and content, and who are rarely seen in the library, workshop or studio outside lecture hours, may well surprise both lecturers and themselves by devoting free time to research and display. A second advantage arising from the students' own experience on group work is that they are able to see the particular areas at which organization is needed and to appreciate for themselves the needs and feelings of those being organized.

It is of course necessary that the students' own experience of group work should be as far as possible comparable with the children's, and hence tutors must take care to ensure that none of the organizational steps is omitted. Moreover, the students' topics may well be undertaken in areas that they will then use in their own work with children. For this reason, it is useful for the tutors organizing the course to offer a wide variety of areas in the first instance, so that students may choose to work at a topic within an area that they expect to use on subsequent group work themselves.

At the time of writing, for example, a hundred and forty students have just finished their own group work in college, having devoted nominally two periods a week over eight weeks to it, though in fact they devoted far more of their own free time to this activity than the allotted timetable time. Four broad topic areas were suggested in the first place by the tutors concerned: historical and environmental studies of the city in which the college is situated; social surveys of different aspects of the city's life; a dramatic production based on some aspect of the history of education; and an investigation into the effects of streaming. These four areas were outlined briefly and students asked to make a preliminary choice by placing three of the four in order of preference. The students then met together in groups according to their first choice and discussed with a tutor how the different topics might be developed. At this stage the allocation to topics was kept flexible, so that students would be free to change their topics if they had second thoughts.

Discussions within these large groups enabled some overall plan to be drawn up, and at this stage there was a certain amount of movement between groups. Soon, however, the larger groups settled down and began to arrange themselves into smaller working groups. By the end of the second week, the smaller groups had been formed and the topic work proper had begun.

Now that the topic work has ended, the students are preparing to make preliminary visits to schools in which they will themselves conduct group work, under the joint supervision of their tutors and experienced teachers. From the initial scheme which they have proposed it is evident that their own topic work has in many cases provided a starting point for their group-work proposals in school.

Thus, in himself undergoing preliminary group work the student may work through some of the fields which he will subsequently base his own teaching plans on, and he will at the same time become aware of the problems of organization from the pupils' own point of view.

THE RELATION OF THE STUDENT'S OWN EXPERIENCE TO THE ORGANIZATION OF GROUP WORK

This brings us to a problem which we cannot pretend we have solved. One of the aims of the students' own group work is that they should become aware of its organizational needs 'from the inside', as it were. At what time and in what way this awareness should be made self-conscious, and translated into plans for future action, is a matter that we have discussed a good deal. Often the most important lessons are essentially those of the moment, which lose much in recollection. For example, when actually faced with a choice of topics, students may decide upon their preferences according to various criteria which—with a certain amount of questioning at the time—they may be able to make explicit. Once the choice has been made, however, and the student is embarked upon the actual work, it is usually extremely difficult for him to remember the manifest reasons for his preference, and virtually impossible to remember those reasons— equally important—which were not actually formulated. Yet an understanding of the various reasons behind the choice of topics gives the student insight into dealing with children's choice situations. Similarly, a student's own reactions to a tutor's interference with his plans—whether that interference is accidental or deliberate—provides a valuable guide to the likely reactions of children to similar interference, but again it is a lesson which can only be learnt at the time, since the memory of it will quickly fade in the activity of the work itself (unless, of course, the tutor continues to interfere!).

In our experience, students are rarely sufficiently psychologically sophisticated to welcome the kind of self-analytical sessions which might enable them to express their reactions to a given situation, to draw teaching conclusions from them, and then to continue in the situation. One way by which we have attempted to overcome this difficulty is by brief periods of suspended activity when students are asked to write short accounts of their reactions to a given situation (for example, how they felt when some limitation on freedom of choice of topic was announced). The fact that tutors do not read these personal and private accounts may encourage some students to be more self-analytical and less defensive than they may otherwise have been. At the end of their own group work, the students are asked to write a short critical essay on some aspect of its organization, and are encouraged to draw upon these accounts as source data.

This is not to say, of course, that students suffer total amnesia regarding their own feelings during the period of their group work, and in discussing it afterwards tutors are often able to remind them of their reactions. However, it remains the case that because the work itself is often so absorbing, temporary setbacks and frustrations tend to be forgotten, so that the same student who protested loudly when it was suggested that he should change topic groups in order to achieve a better balance of numbers, may well be found later on making exactly the same suggestion to his children, and then looking blank when reminded of his own reactions to the identical situation.

THE TIMING OF SUGGESTIONS FOR THE ORGANIZATION OF GROUP WORK

Another difficult problem is that of deciding upon the best time to make available suggestions for the organization of the students' own work with children. We have found that such suggestions have very little meaning for students until they are actually faced with the need for organization and even then it is often not until they have—for example—tried to divide their pupils into groups that they see the difficulties involved. Again, this lack of imagination proceeds from the unfamiliarity of the group-work situation in itself. Having experienced formal lessons they are well aware of what can go wrong and are anxious for guidance on how to avoid it. With group work, however, the problems are not for the most part anticipated and consequently suggestions for dealing with them do not have much meaning beforehand.

This problem is aggravated by the fact that it may only be through their own mistakes in organization that students are able to learn effectively how best to organize. In this situation one must consider not only the effects of those mistakes upon the students, but also their effects upon the children they are teaching, not to mention the wear and tear on the supervisors. At the end of a disorganized and chaotic day a student may well announce that he now realizes the need for giving thought beforehand to this or that aspect of the work, but does this discovery justify the children's experiences?

Moreover, one may be reluctant (as indeed the writers are) to offer specific and detailed advice in the methods of group work for the same reason that one hesitates to lay down the law about any method. As with more formal teaching, in group work a teacher follows those methods which best suit his own personality, and the particular needs of the children he is dealing with; in other words, he develops a personal style. With a good teacher, such a personal style is in fact an extension of his own personality, adapted to the particular circumstances of the classroom; he feels perfectly at home in his methods, and is able to behave naturally because what he is doing is part of his customary mode of expression. This naturalness in turn leads to a natural relationship with the pupils, who respond to the person rather than to the teacher, and in such a way a straightforward, easy warmth is built up between them which is the basis of an enduring rapport. To make over-detailed suggestions is to hinder the development of this rapport because the student seeks to adapt a number of ready-made solutions, instead of starting from basic principles and trying to work through to an individual solution. It is the difference between trying to make a jacket from an assortment of arms, collars, pockets, shoulders, etc., from ready-made garments of different sizes and materials, and making a jacket to fit from a length of cloth.

The writers have tried to overcome this particular problem by offering suggestions relating to essential principles and leaving the detailed implementation of them to the students themselves. (This approach is often looked upon with disfavour by the students, more particularly the lazy ones, who feel that they are being meanly deprived of the very rules they are seeking.) These suggestions are given in the form of written notes after the students' first preliminary visit to schools when they become aware of the problems of organization, and while there is still time for consideration of different ways of solving them.

Supplementary to these notes, talks and demonstrations on particular problems of group work—for example, the formation of groups, the organization of visits, display techniques—are given at different times during the progress of the work itself. Attendance at such talks and demonstrations is, of course, voluntary.

THE ORGANIZATION OF A COURSE ON GROUP WORK

It may be of interest to readers to know how the course at one college was organized, though we would emphasize that we are far from convinced that our present organization is the best, and we offer this account more by way of a critical starting-point.

The course at present contains about a hundred and fifty students preparing for some secondary teaching (including those who are preparing also for work in junior schools, and those who have in mind the possibility of middle schools, with an age-range of 9-13). These students are on the second year of their three-year course. During the first year they undertook a block teaching practice in the kind of school in which they hope to find a job when they leave college and their lesson preparation was orientated towards the kind of teaching they may fairly be expected to do in that job: for junior teachers this has already involved a certain amount of topic work, while for secondary teachers the emphasis has been on what we might call 'enlightened' traditional class teaching.

The second year of their education course has—as far as the method side is concerned—an emphasis on experiments in new approaches, and the group work is part of this emphasis. For the first eight weeks of the autumn term the students are offered a number of topic areas within which to work with an education tutor. After this choice has been made, the tutors proceed as with a class of secondary children: the students are divided into working groups, again by choice; roles and tasks are assigned within the groups; plans for the work are discussed and decided upon; materials, visits, research, etc., are ordered and arranged; the progress of the work is recorded; and, in the eighth week, a display is held of what has been achieved. From time to time the tutor may require his students to stop work for a while and examine their own reactions, or the results of a particular form of organization, but for the most part they are working in the way that children in a class engaged on a group-work topic would work.

Running parallel with their own group work are several courses: a lecture course on indirect methods of teaching, with films and references to various teaching experiments; a lecture-and-demonstration course on the creative use of modern teaching aids, such as the overhead projector, closed-circuit television, etc., and other more academic courses. In addition to their groups for the topic work, the students are also organized into different groups of about seven each, for the discussion of points raised on the academic courses. As these discussion groups are autonomous, and function without the presence of a tutor for the most part, they offer additional experience of working in groups, although the work in this case is purely theoretical discussion, and is not directly linked to any activity.

During the eight weeks of topic work, arrangements are made for the placing of students in schools the following term. Those secondary schools in the area which have taken part in the scheme are invited to offer classes in which the students can work. Teachers offer classes, specifying the age and academic ability of the children, and the subject areas within which the students should work. They also indicate if there are particular parts of the syllabus which should be covered. Towards the end of the topic work, these details from the schools are displayed on the students' notice board (though without the names of the schools), and the students are invited to submit schemes to match them, or alternatively to submit schemes according to their own interests. They are urged themselves to form groups of three to six, but those who are prepared to work in any group can simply state what kind of topics they would like to take part in.

The groups of students, together with groups formed out of the few unattached students, are then required to discuss their proposals with education tutors and also with subject tutors in the various subject areas involved. At this stage, modifications may be suggested to make the schemes more realistic. There then follows a matching of students' schemes and schools' details, after which education tutors visit the schools to discuss the suitability of proposals with the teachers concerned. So far we have been extremely fortunate in that with very few exceptions we have been able to place the students in schools for them to try out the schemes they propose.

By this time the students' own topic work has ended. They visit the schools on the first of a series of three preliminary visits, to meet the teachers and to discuss the feasibility of their schemes with them. The question of the availability of materials, and the possibility of visits, surveys and other outside activities are also considered.

If the teachers accept the schemes as feasible, which—with some modifications—they normally do, the students then begin to fill in the details, again with further consultation with tutors. They are now required to obtain the definite sponsorship of one or more subject tutors in the relevant fields. They are also given some suggestions on the organization of the work they propose, and the lessons to be drawn from their own experience of the topic work are stressed.

There is a particular difficulty here, and it is that the students' understandable anxiety to plan as fully as possible, often coupled with their own enthusiasm and imagination, tends to lead to too detailed planning, with insufficient provision for the children's participation and ideas. This is, of course, a legacy from their experience of teacher-directed lessons, and indeed reflects the lesson they have learnt themselves during their first teaching practice of the need, in a traditional lesson, to have all the details well planned in advance. This is, in our experience, perhaps the most difficult single problem in training students in group-work methods. Because of their uncertainty about the approach, because of their fear that the children will not respond to the opportunities offered to them, or because the students themselves get carried away by their own enthusiasm, they tend to prepare in far too great detail, with the result that the areas of choice and initiative open to the children become so limited as to endanger the value of the whole approach. The way in which we ourselves try to overcome this difficulty is to stress to the students the need to concentrate in their preparation on procedures, rather than on content. We have found that if a student has determined before the lesson the ways in which, say, groups are to be formed, or decisions taken, and has made provision for a number of alternatives according to what happens, this goes a long way to allaying his anxiety about giving the children some freedom of choice. There is also much to be said for the students being asked to devise a fair number of alternatives in the actual content of the work; this has the double merit of providing a store of ideas on which to draw should the children be unusually slow in coming forward with their own, and also it prevents the student from being committed to one particular topic for which his own enthusiasm might outrun the need to give the children some initiative.

The students are expected to work each with a group of 4-8 children, which means between three and six students to a class. They are expected to prepare schemes jointly which they can present to the class as a whole for preliminary discussions, and which can then be divided into topics on each of which one student can work with his or her own group, reporting back to

the whole class from time to time. In this way, the students get
to know a small number of children extremely well. Not only
do they discover how such a group—given sufficient initiative—
can work for itself, but also they come to know the children
as individuals, each with his or her own strengths and weaknesses.
This, it is hoped, gives the students the confidence to embark
on group work with a whole class, when they come to their
next block teaching practice in the following term. And of course,
the students take it in turn to deal with the whole class when
they are arranging the preliminary discussions and the reporting
back sessions.

Three preliminary visits are made in all, enabling the students
to take full advantage of discussions with the teachers, to make
careful preparations for materials and other facilities, and to
meet the children to discuss their plans.

The group work itself occupies a morning a week throughout
the spring term. Education and subject tutors visit the schools
to discuss with the teachers and students the progress of the
work. Tutorials are held in college with individuals, and occasional talks and demonstrations are given on different aspects of
organization of the work. In addition there are lecture courses on
the social psychology of small groups, and the teaching of educationally sub-normal children; attendance at all these lectures is
voluntary.

The group work finishes at the end of the spring term with a
working conference of tutors and teachers. Reference has already
been made to the recommendations made at one such conference,
which are reproduced below in the Appendix.[1]

During the Summer term an attempt is made to give the
students an opportunity to think about the theoretical aims implicit in group work and in other experimental methods, and this
leads up to a short block teaching practice, unsupervised by the
college, during which students are encouraged to experiment for
themselves. As part of their experimentation it is suggested that
they should embark upon some form of group work with at

[1] See below, p. 123.

least one of their classes. This time, of course, they will have to take responsibility for the whole class. It is hoped that their own experience of topic work, followed by the previous term's work with small groups, will have given them sufficient confidence to do so.

8 Conclusions

GROUP WORK NOT A UNIVERSAL TEACHING METHOD

We have said earlier that both the content and the methods of the traditional secondary-school curriculum are today under criticism. Many teachers and educationalists are dissatisfied with the present state of secondary education and are re-examining its principles and practice. Experiments are in progress in organization, in curricula, and in teaching methods, and these cross-fertilize each other and contribute to a general state of willingness to question even the most basic assumptions. The influence of the Nuffield teaching projects, for example, is felt well beyond the boundaries of the subjects with which they are concerned. Teachers and heads who try out new forms of school or class organization are no longer regarded as cranks, but are invited to talk at conferences, and their schools are visited by keenly interested colleagues. That a good deal of present-day experiment is carried out within the state system is itself a sign of the changed ethos within which we work.

One of the dangers of general dissatisfaction with any state of things is the tendency for some new idea, which can be shown to lead to some kind of improvement, to be seized upon and taken up as a universal cure to all ills. We should be quite misunderstood if we were thought to be recommending group work as some such universal solution to the problems of secondary education. Certainly we feel that it should become a normal part of the secondary teacher's repertoire, and we would argue that, as an approach, it can be successfully used in a wide variety of teaching situations with children of all ages, not excluding sixth-formers. But we would be opposed to its adoption as the

GWSS—E

sole teaching method for any pupils, just as we would oppose the adoption of any other single method. Not only do children need the stimulation of a variety of ways of learning, but also different learning situations may well demand different approaches, and the skilled teacher is the one with both a variety of methods at his command and the discernment to know which is appropriate for any given pupil on any given occasion. Moreover, group work has its limitations, some of which have already been touched upon, and it would seem appropriate to end this brief account by discussing these in a little more detail and by suggesting some means by which they may be overcome.

GROUP WORK AND 'DISCIPLINE'

Before doing so, however, there is one objection which is sometimes raised to group work but which, we feel, proceeds from a mistaken understanding of its nature. This objection is expressed in various ways, nearly all of which include the emotive word 'discipline'. For example, it may be argued that to allow children to pursue their own investigations may arouse their interest, but they will never in this way benefit from the 'discipline' a subject imposes. Or, alternatively, it may be put that what is valuable in subject teaching is not so much the content itself as the 'discipline' of learning methodically, rigorously and painstakingly. (This last argument, incidentally, includes a variant of the old transfer of training fallacy.)

Now it seems to us that these and similar arguments are based upon the false supposition that learning through personal investigation—which is what group work entails—is necessarily undisciplined; that is, unmethodical and superficial. Such a supposition is totally unwarranted, as anyone who has himself undertaken research must be forced to admit. The comparison between research work and the investigations of group work is not farfetched. For it is from precisely the same kind of intellectual curiosity and excitement that motivates a research worker, albeit at a different level, that group work draws its incentive. And just as a research worker discovers that, if his findings are to be sufficiently valid to allow him to pursue his researches further, he must refine his techniques and develop a high degree of self-criticism, so do the members of a group investigating some topic which has fired their interest discover that they must work carefully and methodically if they are to satisfy their curiosity. What is immediately apparent in the classroom is that the same children who are content with careless work when they are doing tasks set by the teacher will expect very much higher standards from each other, and will accept these standards for themselves, when they are self-directed.

In other words, not only does group work have its own discipline, but that discipline is self-engendered. We would submit that the development of the capacity for such self-engendered discipline is one of the proper aims of education and one which must be preferred to the alternative aim of inculcating discipline through imitation, habit or fear.

There is a further, and in our view equally invalid, criticism made of group work, which is really little more than an extension of the foregoing. Children when they grow up have to learn to adjust themselves to a hard world, this argument runs, and so they should be forced to endure hardship as children so that they become habituated to it. 'We all have to do things we don't want to, so we might as well get used to the experience while we are young,' is another way of putting it—a viewpoint that reveals a sad inability to recognize that whether a task involves pleasure or drudgery often depends as much on the motivation of the doer as it does on the nature of the task itself. Cleaning a room in expectation of a visit from a loved one can be a joyous activity while the identical task done at the orders of a hated master can be misery. The successful businessman takes a delight in the calculation that the ill paid clerk finds irksome almost beyond endurance. Surely our aim is to produce in our children the capacity to work hard and to work well, not because their sensitivities have become dulled and their feelings blunted, but because they have had experience of the joy of achievement. That experience is a direct function of the degree of personal responsibility for the task achieved and can never be felt in its pure form by those who simply do what they are told, however much they are rewarded by praise, stars, merit marks or any of the other substitutes for curiosity and invention.

ORGANIZATION AND THE TEACHER'S ROLE

There are, however, some problems raised by critics of group work which appear to have a greater validity than these, and in particular certain questions of organization remain. Before discussing these, we must stress that the success with which group work is carried out depends, ultimately, upon the quality of the teacher—upon his enthusiasm, sympathetic understanding of the children's difficulties, and upon the thought and care which he puts into the preparation which is still necessary—and this of course applies no matter what method is used.

As with all teaching, up to a certain point, the more favourable the pupil/teacher ratio the better. This is also the case where group-work methods are used, and we would like to make the point that we do not envisage this method of working as a substitute for teachers. Indeed, as has already been demonstrated elsewhere in this book, where there is inadequate or desultory teacher participation, the whole value is undermined. The teacher cannot abrogate his responsibilities for the learning that is carried on by pupils under his care but must be available for consultation and to give support as and when needed. He must also organize the flow of materials, negotiate the occasional or regular use of art, practical or other rooms for individuals or groups of children and organize them on visits outside the school, if the rules require it.

It has already been said that he should aim to act as a sounding board rather than as an initiator, but even so he will periodically need to help a group to redirect its thinking into more profitable channels when they have exhausted a line of inquiry or reached an impasse. To be able to do this means he must be in effective contact with each group's activities and plans. Otherwise he will be in danger of being unable to contribute without actually imposing his own ideas.

Some teachers may prefer to hold discussions with groups on their work at regular intervals. It may be argued that this has value at the outset, but care must be exercised or the teacher will find that there will be a temptation for the group to seek approval at every step. This, of course, would defeat the object of the exercise. More than this, it would inhibit the ultimate transfer of responsibility for learning on the part of the child, from the teacher to the child himself. Such a transfer of this kind can only occur when the initiative and direction of a project are wholly controlled by the group and the teacher's role is minimal. This does not mean that the teacher thereby becomes redundant. It is precisely because of his availability that the children feel able to initiate and carry out the work. But they remain children and we must not think that they will, as children, accept full responsibility for the conditions of their learning, nor is it proper that they should be expected to do so.

The most appropriate level of participation on the part of the teacher will vary from group to group, and from teacher to teacher and will have to be learned by the teacher himself to fit different situations, topics and children. And in particular, the special needs of individual children still have to be met by the teacher.

It is our experience that, once the work is under way, this method increases the opportunities for direct and personal contact. Because children are sharing experience, learning and discovering in small groups, the measure of security felt by the individual is increased and there is less need for either conflict or submissive dependence upon teacher as authority. The 'authority' in the situation is vested in the group itself of which the child is also a member and thus he can influence decisions. Where there is a good measure of participation and internal democracy the teacher is not even part of that authority in the sense that he seeks to impose his will upon others. Submissive and over-dependent children will gain from their closer, more intimate relationship with other children within the smaller working groups, a greater measure of security than from the large class unit. At the same time, their own contribution to the smaller group will have a greater significance both for the workings of the others and for themselves. What is more, the teacher will find opportunities to approach such children more personally on their own level of interest and through their own work.

In the case of the dominant child, the teacher's role may well need to be a more active one. A domineering child will probably try to direct the activities of the group of which he is a member. If he also happens to be an able child, there will be a very real temptation to leave him to get on with it! On the other hand, if this happens, the teacher might as well have continued with the direct-teaching methods as before. The problem here arises as to how to relieve the group from an overbearing influence, without either taking sides or being unduly harsh. In such a situation we have found that others in the group will often follow up questions, put initially by the teacher to the dominant one, which either show up weaknesses in his own plans, or give expression to another point of view. Having made the point, the teacher can withdraw and return later at some propitious moment to gauge whether a new balance has been struck or whether further action is needed by him.

The point is, that he will be called upon to use his professional skill, experience, understanding and knowledge constantly, but in a variety of ways, according to the single individual or group of individuals he is with at any particular time.

These demands will evoke new skills which, as with former skills, will have to be learned and used with varying degrees of refinement.

The children themselves will become increasingly familiar with this method of working as they make their way through the secondary school and it is hoped they will change their own approach to group membership, examining the group more in relation to the task in hand and the qualities of the individual members in terms of the requirements of the task, than in terms of friendship alone. When this happens, it may well be argued that a new growth dimension has been reached, because what is implicit in such choice is a willingness to adapt one's own feelings, behaviour and approach to another individual in order to complete successfully a worthwhile task.

This seems to us to be a very worthy aim of group work—an aim entirely relevant to the realities of life after school in the day to day world of commerce, industry and the professions, where adjustment is constantly required.

In this context, at least, the group-work method of teaching would appear to be a very satisfactory method of educating for the future of the child.

Appendix

The following summaries are of discussions between tutors and teachers engaged in supervising students on group work. These discussions formed part of an evaluative conference held at the end of a year's experimental programme.

I. THE RELEVANCE OF GROUP WORK FOR THE SECONDARY TEACHER

1. *How successful is work of this kind for secondary children?*
   It was felt that success depends on a number of factors, including:
   (a) the degree to which this approach reflects the approach adopted in the school as a whole;
   (b) related to this, how far the school organization facilitates the work, e.g., through block timetabling and the provision of adequate space and equipment; block timetabling can provide adequate sessions of work (it was felt that $1\frac{1}{2}$ hours constitutes the minimum period of work for satisfactory progress to be maintained) and makes team teaching possible; several teachers working in this way can share their knowledge and experience in developing appropriate techniques;
   (c) the amount of experience the children have already had in this kind of work; it was felt that they gain more as they master the relevant basic skills;
   (d) the degree to which the teacher can accept the role of someone sharing the learning experience with the children, rather than that of the authoritative source of knowledge.

2. *How far is it applicable to children of all abilities and age ranges?*
   (a) There was fairly general agreement that some kind of

group work might be applicable at any age. Some felt that such work is more appropriate to less able children; that more able children prefer to work on their own. Others questioned this distinction and argued that all children can benefit from this work: it has certainly been carried out successfully with able children. In group work children learn from one another and this does not mean merely that the less able learn from the more able.

(b) It was felt by some that practical skills cannot be learnt in this way but must be mastered first, before they can be applied in group activities. There was, however, some feeling that any such necessary formal work might best arise from a felt need during group activities and thus be more purposeful as a result.

3. *How far is the experience for the student of relevance to his ultimate responsibility for the whole class?*

(a) It was agreed that it is not easy for anyone to take a whole class in this way, especially initially, but that it is possible to develop appropriate techniques with experience.

(b) There was general agreement that there is a considerable gap between taking a small group and having responsibility for an entire class working in this way, and it was felt that the present training of teachers does not bridge it adequately. It was suggested that a step towards this might be to encourage students to take responsibility for the whole class in turn during the last few weeks of their project. The second year 'unsupervised' practice might also provide opportunities for a student to attempt this, provided that the school was sympathetic and understood the problems.

4. *How much freedom should be given to the children and students as far as the syllabus is concerned?*

It was agreed that the motivation of both students and the children is important and that the momentum gained when they are pursuing a topic of special interest to them is valuable. It was argued, however, that while some subjects (such as English and history) are 'capacious' and lend themselves to divergence, others (such as language and mathematics) are 'linear' and do not permit much. There seemed to be general agreement that languages present a special case, but there was less agreement concerning other subjects; certainly group work has been successfully applied in teaching mathematics. In part at least this problem depends upon the nature of the syllabus—how much stress there is on the acquisition of specific items of knowledge. One solution that works in some contexts is for the teacher to allow great freedom initially and then to guide the work into channels that will fill in the essential gaps afterwards. If the teacher knows where he wants the investigation to lead there is much he can do to lead it in the appropriate direction without imposing the direction from above; but he should be ready to accept unexpected developments and to evaluate them objectively.

II. THE SUITABILITY OF PROJECTS FOR GROUP WORK

1. *What do the children get from group work? How can projects best be organized for children to get the most benefit?*

   (a) It was agreed that the benefits to children taking part in group work were social as well as academic, particularly with regard to the opportunity for the informal expression of opinions. It was felt, however, that there was a danger of more able children moving ahead in their own work within the project and leaving the rest behind; this was more likely with inexperienced students, who might respond to the efforts of the abler children, while failing to recognize the lack of participation of others. For this reason it was suggested that students should be carefully prepared for group work, preferably being attached to teachers with experience of this method. It was also agreed that students require a careful briefing on the kinds of projects that children of all abilities were likely to work best with, and that they should be made aware of the special difficulties some children might find in regard to given skills and/or subjects.

(b) It was suggested that at least one student in each group should be a specialist in one of the areas in which the project was likely to be mainly centred.

(c) It was agreed that sufficient time must be made available for work on projects to enable the student to make provisions for visits and other activities likely to canalize and sustain interest in the work.

(d) It was agreed that sufficient financial provision should be made well beforehand to prevent worthwhile projects from collapsing from want of materials.

2. *What kinds of projects are most suitable in general terms? In terms of different age-ranges and abilities?*

(a) It was agreed that group work should provide opportunities for the exercise of as much choice as possible in order to generate enthusiasm and involvement, but at the same time it is necessary to relate the work to a central theme in order that children's work can be interrelated. In this connection, the students' careful preparation is of the utmost importance.

(b) It was felt that students should not be given remedial classes where specialist experience is necessary.

(c) It was felt that too great an ability range within a group of children might create difficulties.

(d) It was felt that third- and fourth-year classes were often the most suitable for group work, followed by first and second years.

III. THE ORGANIZATION OF GROUP WORK

1. *Time needed (a) in the classroom? (b) in overall duration?*

(a) Members agreed that a single teaching period was inadequate for work of this kind and that, although a double period may be adequate for work of a more limited nature to be carried out within the school, it was desirable to devote a whole morning or afternoon to group work whenever possible, especially when outside activities and visits formed part of the scheme.

It was acknowledged that if half a day was allocated for work of this kind, timetabling difficulties might arise when the work was over and the students withdrew. A suggestion was made that if the school allocated the group-work time wholly within a single year, the difficulty could be minimized, particularly where team-teaching methods could be used.

(b) An apprenticeship period for students was regarded as being useful if the class and teacher were not already familiar with group-working methods. This was also a useful time for students to become acquainted with the children and school situation within which they were to work later. For this reason together with that of likely timetable difficulties being created, it was held that it would be undesirable for students to serve their apprenticeship with one class but carry out their own work with another.

2. *Best time of year for work?*

The majority view was that the Spring Term was the best for this work. Although it was agreed that for a certain type of project the Summer Term was more appropriate, it was held that the school exams., adventure activities, school holidays and camps normally held in the Summer Term would seriously hamper the students' efforts.

3. *Size of groups?*

Student pupil ratios were agreed as follows: —

1 student to 8 where the pupils were older and more able.
1 „ „ 6 for middle streams.
1 „ „ 4 for younger or remedial groups.

It was recommended that students should be free to choose work with remedial groups if they so wished, but that they should be made to realize that the work would be of a different nature involving more individual teaching. Where opportunities exist for students to work with groups of mixed ability it was held that it would be valuable for them to do so provided that the range was not too great.

4. *Student/teacher allocation?*

Teachers felt that students could usefully be allocated to schools on the basis of four students to one teacher although the number would vary according to the type of work to be done and the facilities available, and some could accommodate up to six students.

5. *Display and storage*

The maximum possible space should be made available for display, and cupboard room made available for materials to be used.

Although exhibition and display of work was considered to be desirable it was held that it should not be allowed to become the aim of the work and that much of value would be accomplished that could not be displayed or exhibited.

IV. THE SUPERVISION OF GROUP WORK

1. *Students' needs*

   (a) It is necessary for students to make early contact with the schools in which they are to do their group work. A minimum of two preliminary visits is suggested; during the first visit the student should obtain a general view of the school, and should meet, as far as possible, all the teachers interested in group work. For subsequent preliminary visits the student should bring his draft proposals for the scheme work or projects he hopes to carry out, to discuss the feasibility of this with the teachers concerned. He should also have a fair idea of what might be needed in the way of materials and other resources, so that the availability of these in the school can be checked, and orders placed if necessary.

(b) In all preliminary planning, students should be required to make their own projections and estimates of what will be needed. Where students are co-operating in the first instance with teachers' schemes, they should be involved purposefully in the planning from the first.

(c) The suggested number of pupils per student in a group is 4-8; the suggested number of groups per teacher is 3-5; this gives an outside maximum of 40 children engaged in any given group-work activity.

2. *Supervision by teachers*

(a) Teachers should guide students in the same way that, ideally, the students should be guiding their pupils— that is, not by direct instruction, but by raising questions. Very often it is necessary to do no more than ask the questions; the children will want to find out the answers, and the good student will try to suggest ways, or ask the children to suggest ways, in which they can do so.

(b) Supervising teachers, may, if necessary, supplement the work of students if it is felt that the essential parts of the syllabus are being omitted.

(c) It is often necessary to allow students to make mistakes in order to learn, and supervising teachers should be prepared for this to happen. For this reason, projects which entail expensive materials, or essential works, may not be suitable for group work by students.

(d) In the same way that supervising teachers should avoid doing the work for the students, they should see that the students do not do the work for the children. If the children are to obtain full value from group work, they must play a responsible part in the activities, and supervising teachers should guide students to allow them to do so.

(e) Teachers should require students to plan well ahead, particularly with regard to the need for materials, apparatus, transport, permits, etc., but again they should not do the ordering, writing or planning for them unless absolutely necessary. Students will learn the need for careful organization only by being made responsible for it. However, teachers must exercise overall supervision especially where excursions outside the school are being made.

3. *College tutors*
    (a) College tutors should confer regularly with the supervising teacher, with the knowledge of the students, to show the students that their work is being recognized and to iron out supervisory problems.
    (b) A meeting of the supervising teacher, tutor and students outside the classroom should be arranged at least once during the group work, to enable an overall evaluation of the projects in hand to be made.
    (c) Supervising teachers should have copies of recommendations given to students by the college.

4. *School arrangements*
    Schools need to know by Easter the preceding year what days and times have been fixed for group work so that timetables can be blocked out.

V. THE ASSESSMENT OF GROUP WORK

1. *How can group-work projects be assessed?*
    The group considered that conventional achievement tests are not by themselves a satisfactory means of assessing group-work projects in so far as they measure only academic attainment, neglecting such significant variables as the children's enjoyment and the improved communication between pupils and teacher. It was felt that participation in group projects was of value for all children and was particularly appropriate to 'Newsom' children. (The term *project* itself was not, however, acceptable to all members of the group.)

2. *How can the children's progress be assessed?*
Again, it was felt that there is no easily applied single yardstick. The group considered the extent to which the pupils' gain in personality and as members of the community—important aspects of group work—should be included in any assessment of progress as well as academic achievement. It was pointed out that the pupils were making progress not only in the subject matter but also in the new approach to learning itself. An appraisal of progress should include the work done, whether in display, collection, taped oral work, records or the like.

3. *How can the students' progress be assessed?*
The group felt that these group-work experiences enabled the students, in a comparatively short time, to attain a good relationship with the pupils, one of mutual respect and understanding. The students gained much from their experience in practical work management and organization. The amount of preparation and prior research could easily be judged, but again overall assessment was not straightforward.

4. *What is the place of the students' logbooks?*
The group felt that the logbooks would give evidence of the drive coming from the students and assure that an overall plan and pattern underlay the work.

References and books for further reading

ANDERSON, H. H. & BREWER, H. M. (1945-6), *Studies of Teachers' Classroom Personalities: Applied Psychology Monographs of the American Association for Applied Psychology*, Nos. 6, 8 and 11. New York, Stanford University Press.

BANY, M. A. & JOHNSON, L. V. (1964), *Classroom Group Behaviour: Group Dynamics in Education*, New York, Collier-Macmillan.

BARKER, R. *et al* (*Ed.*) (1943), *Child Behaviour and Development*, New York, McGraw-Hill.

BAVELAS, A. (1942), 'Morale and the Training of Leaders' in WATSON (1942).

BERENDA, R. (1950), *The Influence of the Group on the Judgments of Children*, New York, Teachers College, Columbia University.

BERKOWITZ, L. (*Ed.*) (1964), *Advances in Experimental Social Psychology*, Vol. I, New York, Academic Press.

BION, W. R. (1961), *Experiences in Groups and other papers*, London, Tavistock.

BRADFORD, L. P. *et al.* (*Ed.*) (1964), *T-Group Theory and Laboratory Method*, New York, Wiley.

CARTWRIGHT, D. & ZANDER, A. (*Ed.*) (1960), *Group Dynamics: Research and Theory*, 2nd edition, New York, Harper.

CARY, J. (1947), *Mister Johnson*, London, Michael Joseph.

References 133

Cook, H. C. (1919), *The Play Way*, London, Heinemann.

Deutsch, M. (1949), 'The Effects of Co-operation and Competition on Group Process', *Human Relations*, V, pp. 129-52 & 199-232.

Education, Ministry of (1963), *Half Our Future* (The Newsom Report), London, H.M.S.O.

Education and Science, Dept. of (1967), *Children and their Primary Schools* (The Plowden Report), London H.M.S.O.

Evans, K. M. (1962), *Sociometry and Education*, London, Routledge & Kegan Paul.

Fleming, C. E. (*Ed.*) (1951), *Studies in the Social Psychology of Adolescence*, London, Routledge & Kegan Paul.

Freud, A. (1937), *The Ego and the Mechanisms of Defence*, London, Hogarth.

Gronlund, N. E. (1959), *Sociometry in the Classroom*, New York, Harper.

Hare, A. P. (1962), *Handbook of Small Group Research*, Glencoe, Illinois, Free Press.

Hare, A. P. *et al.* (1965), *Small Groups: Studies in Social Interaction*, Revised edition, New York, Knopf.

Holt, J. (1964), *How Children Fail*, London, Pitman.

Hughes, T. (n.d.), *Tom Brown's Schooldays*, London, Epworth.

Inhelder, B. & Piaget, J. (1958), *The Growth of Logical Thinking from Childhood to Adolescence*, translated by Anne Parsons and Stanley Milgram, New York, Basic Books.

134 *References*

JACKSON, B. (1964), *Streaming: an Education System in Miniature*, London, Routledge & Kegan Paul.

JAQUES, E. (1951), *The Changing Culture of a Factory*, London, Tavistock.

LAMMING, G. (1953), *In the Castle of My Skin*, London, Michael Joseph.

LEWIN, R., LIPPITT, R. & WHITE, R. K. (1939), 'Patterns of Aggressive Behaviour in Experimentally Created "Social Climates." ' *Journal of Social Psychology*, X, pp. 271-99.

LIPPITT, R. (1940), 'An Experimental Study of the Effect of Democratic and Authoritarian Group Atmospheres'. Studies in Topological and Vector Psychology I, *University of Iowa Studies in Child Welfare*, XVI, No. 3.

LIPPITT, R. & WHITE, R. K. (1943), 'The "Social Climate" of Children's Groups', in BARKER *et al.* (1943).

LIPPITT, R. & WHITE, R. K. (1958), 'An Experimental Study of Leadership and Group Life', in MACCOBY *et al.* (1958).

LOCKE, J. (1884), *Some Thoughts Concerning Education*, Edited by R. H. Quick. Revised edition, Cambridge University Press.

LUMSDAINE, A. A. & GLASER, R. (1960), *Teaching Machines and Programmed Learning*, Washington, D.C., National Educational Association, Department of Audio-Visual Instruction.

MACCOBY, E. E. *et al.* (*Ed.*) (1958), *Readings in Social Psychology*, 3rd edition, New York, Holt, Rinehart & Winston.

MACKENZIE, R. F. (1965), *Escape From the Classroom*, London, Collins.

MARSHALL, S. (1963), *An Experiment in Education*, Cambridge University Press.

MAYO, L. (1949), *The Social Problems of an Industrial Civilization*, London, Routledge & Kegan Paul.

MILLS, T. M. (1964), *Group Transformation: an analysis of a learning group*, New Jersey, Prentice-Hall.

MORENO, J. L. (1934), *Who Shall Survive?* Washington, Nervous & Mental Disease Pub. Co.

OESER, O. A. (*Ed.*) (1960), *Teacher, Pupil and Task: Elements of Social Psychology applied to Education*, 2nd edition, London, Tavistock.

OTTAWAY, A. K. C. (1966), *Learning through Group Experience*, London, Routledge & Kegan Paul.

PLATO (1951), *The Symposium*, translated by W. Hamilton. London, Penguin.

RICHARDSON, J. L. (1951), 'Group Relations and Education', Chapter 1 of FLEMING (1951).

ROWE, A. D. (1959), *The Education of the Average Child*, London, Harrap.

SCHOOLS COUNCIL (1966), *Raising the School-Leaving Age*, Working Paper No. 2, London, H.M.S.O.

SHERIF, M. & SHERIF, C. W. (1964), *Reference Groups: Exploration into Conformity and Deviation of Adolescents*, New York, Harper & Row.

SKINNER, B. F. (1960), 'The Science of Learning and the Art of Teaching', in LUMSDAINE & GLASER (1960).

136   *References*

STEINER, R. (1954), *Education and Modern Spiritual Life*, 2nd edition, London, Anthroposophical Society.

STRANG, R. (1958), *Group Work in Education*, 3rd edition, New York, Harper.

TANNER, J. M. (1961), *Education and Physical Growth*, London, University of London Press.

THELEN, H. A. (1954), *Dynamics of Groups at Work*, Chicago, University of Chicago Press.

THELEN, H. A. (1960), *Education and the Human Quest*, New York, Harper & Row.

WATSON, G. (1942), *Civilian Morale*, Boston, Houghton Mifflin.

WHITE, P. (1957), *Voss*, London, Eyre & Spottiswoode.

WHITE, R. K. & LIPPITT, R. (1960), *Autocracy and Democracy: an Experimental Inquiry*, New York, Harper.

WILLMOTT, P. (1966), *Adolescent Boys in East London*, London, Routledge & Kegan Paul.

YATES, A. (Ed.) (1966), *Grouping in Education: a report sponsored by the Unesco Institute for Education, Hamburg*, New York, Wiley.

Index

Abilities, children's, 8, 14-15, 17, 20, 24, **26-7**, 29, 35, 39, 52-3, 120, 123-8, 130
  group work and, vii, 8, 20, 24, 29, 35, 39, 52-3, **123-8**, 130
Able children, 120, 124, 125, 127
Academic attainment, grouping by, 26-8, 29
Academic children, 17
Accuracy, standards of, 74
Achievement tests, 130
Administration, school, 41, 123
Adolescence, psychology of, **75-80**, 82-3, 96, 99-100
  group work appropriate to, 75-80, 82
Adult role, adolescent's preparation for, 82-3
Adults, defiance of, 51, 68-9, 77, 78, 79, 99
Adventure activities, 127
Age of children suitable for group work, 123-4, 126
Aggression, children's, 24, 91-2; see also Hostility, children's
Allocation of tasks in group work, 2, 36, 45, 46, 51-2, 56
  under autocratic methods, 89
Anderson, H. H., 93, 132
Anxiety, children's, 42, 76, 79
  students', 112
Apathy in children, 9, 69, 79, 102; see also Boredom
Apparatus in group work, 32, 41, 56, 129-30
Apprenticeship to group work, 20-1, 125, 127
Approaches to group work, different, 44-7, 61-74, 123
Approval, need for, 87-8, 98-100
Art, 69
Asch, Solomon, 97
Assessment of group work, 57, 130-1; see also Group work, evaluation of
Assignments, individual, 10, 14, 62-4

Attitudes, development of new, 51, 67
Audio-visual aids, 28
Australian aborigines, 59
Authoritarian methods, 53-5, 89-94; see also Teacher, authority of the, and Teacher-directed lessons
Autocracy and Democracy, 88, 136
Autocratic leader, the, 53-5, 89-94; see also Teacher, authority of the

Bany, M. A., 100n, 132
Barker, R., 132
Bavelas, A., 93, 132
Below-average ability, children of, 20
Berenda, Ruth, 97, 132
Berkowitz, L., 88n, 94n, 132
Bethel, Maine, 97
Bion, W. R., 98n, 132
Boredom in children, 13, 37, 43-4, 51, 55, 69, 102; see also Apathy
Bradford, L. P., 98n, 132
Brewer, H. M., 93, 132
Bright children, 8
Broadcasts, use of radio and television, 63, 64, 67
Budgeting, 22
Building, 22, 41, 69
Bullying, 68

Capabilities, children's see Abilities, children's
Cartwright, D., 100n, 132
Cary, Joyce, 54, 132
Certificate of Secondary Education, vii, 15, 20, 69
  Mode III, vii, 15
Chairman, role of, 54, 55
Child psychology, 12; see also Psychology of adolescence
Children's abilities, see Abilities, children's

Children's initiative, 7, 31, 38, 39, 41, 90, 96
Children's reactions to group work, 1-11
Children's responsibility for group work, 5, 31, 33-4, 40, 99
Children's suggestions for group work, 39, 43-4, 91
Choice, freedom of, *see* Freedom of choice
Choice of topics, students', 105, 106 111
Class teaching, *see* Teacher-directed lessons
Climbing, 68, 69
Clubs, children's, 55, 88-94
Colleges of education, 10-11, 12, 19-25, 101-14, 123-31
    and schools, co-operation between, 10-11, 19-25, 101-14, 123-31
    courses in, 12, 19-25, 101-14; *see also* Students, training of
Colour problem, play about, 22, 24
Community services, 22, 41
Competition, 7, 86, 94-6
    compared with co-operation, 94-6
Compositions, writing, 62
Concepts, formation of, 80-1
Conclusion of group work, 38, 64
Conference to evaluate a training programme in group-work methods, 24-5, 113, 123-31
Confidence, children's, 5, 7, 32, 40-1, 44, 45, 76, 81, 97
Conformity 24, 77, 96, 97
Conversations, children's 43
Cook, H. Caldwell, 14, 133
Co-operation in group work, children's, 61-4, 79
Co-operation compared with competition, 94-6
Corporal punishment, 84-7
Cost of materials for group work, 32, 56, 126
Courts of law, project on, 3-4
Covering the syllabus under group work, 4, 6, 38, 41, 57, 58, 124-5, 129
Critical attitudes, development of, 33-4, 39, 73-4
Criticism, development of self-, 30, 39, 74, 91, 93
Criticisms of group work, 6, 90, 91

Decorating, interior, 41, 68, 69, 90

Defiance of adults, 51, 68-9, 77, 78, 79, 99
Definition of group work, working, 30
Delinquents, 24, 63
Democratic methods, 53-4, 89-94; *see also*, Majority, wishes of the
Democracy, 55, 65
Dependence on the teacher, children's, 35; *see also* Teacher, authority of the; Teacher-directed lessons
Dependent children, over-, 119
Design, 22, 41
Deutsch, Morton, 94-6, 133
Dickens, Charles, 85
Difficult children, 13, 24, 50, 51, 68-9
Directed teaching, *see* Teacher-directed lessons
Direction, children's self-, 4, 29-30, 37, 51, 67, 80, **83-8**
    versus discipline, 83-8
Discipline, 68-9, 83-8, 116-8
Discussion groups, students', 94-6
Discussion in class, vii, 4, 10, **31-6,** 43-4, 45, 47, 55, 58, 70, 72, 80, 129
    conducting, 43-4, 47, 58, 129
    in group work, 4, 36, **43-4,** 47, 55, 58, 70, 72, 80, 129
    teacher's contribution to, 31-6, 58, 129; *see also* Suggestions, teachers'
Discussion under democratic leadership, 89
    under *laissez-faire* leadership, 89
Display, 23, 38, 45, 59, 60, 128, 131
Disputes in group work, 56
Division of labour in group work, 49, 51, 53; *see also* Allocation of tasks
Dominating children, 9, 53-4, 95, 120
Drama in group work, 3, 5-6, 22, 24, 38, 41, 45, 46, 54, 59, 69
    as a means of instruction, 59
Dress, adolescents', 77

Education, Ministry of, 133
Education, philosophy of, 12
Effect, Law of, 86-8
Efficiency of group work, 75
Electricity, project on, 1, 22, 70-1

Emotions, children's, 4, 75-80, 83-4, 96, 98
Employment, investigation into, 63-4, 72-4
End-product of group work, 39, 40, 52, 54, 55, 60, 128; *see also* Evaluation of group work
English, 125
Enterprise, individual, 96
Evaluation of group work, 24-5, 30, 40, 57-8, 113, 123-31
Evaluative conference on a training programme for group work, 24-5, 113, 123-31
Evans, K. M., 48n, 133
Examinations, 14, 15, 16, 69-74, 82, 127
and group work, 69-74, 82, 127
Excursions, school, 14, 41, 56, 82, 130; *see also* Visits
Exercise, Law of, 33
Exhibitions, 14, 41, 59, 60, 69, 128
in group work, 41, 59, 60, 128
Experience, use of children's, 81
Experiment in Education, An, 60, 134
Experiments in social psychology, 88-100

Facilities for group work, 56-7
Factories, visits to, 56
Family, 76-7
Fears, childrens', 76
Feasibility of group-work schemes, 44, 45, 65, 111, 128
Files, children's, 59
students', 23-4, 131
Film-making, 38, 41
Films, use of, 2, 10, 66, 70
Firms, letters to, 2 57, 70
Fleming, C. E., 88n, 133
Foods, study of, 66
Formal group work, 26
Formal lessons, *see* Teacher-directed lessons
Formation of groups, *see* Groups, formation of
Framework in group work, 2, 4, 5, 6, 42, 65, 83, 102, 103
Freedom in group work, meaning of, 4-5, 124-5
Freedom of choice, children's, 5, 28-9, 31, 35-6, 44-7, 48-52, 112, 126
essential principle of groupwork, 28-9

importance of, 35-6
Freedom to pursue their own interests, children's, 3, 4, 5-6, 60, 67, 68, 70, 87 125
Freud, Anna, 79, 133
Friendliness, children's 91, 92
Friendliness, teacher's need for, 9-10
Friendship as a basis for forming groups, 72, 120
Frustration, children's sense of, 43-4, 61, 76, 91
Fry, Elizabeth, 63

Gangs, children's, 77n
General Certificate of Education, 16
Geography, 63, 67, 71
Geometry, 22
Glaser, R., 134
Gronlund, N. E., 48n, 133
Group dynamics, 97; *see also* Groups, membership of
Group interaction, 90-100; *see also* Groups, membership of
Group leaders, 9, 53-5, 79, 87, 88-94
Group procedure, 53-6
Group teaching, 26-30
Group work, *passim*
abilities, and children's, vii, 8, 20, 24, 29, 35, 39, 52-3, **123-8**, 130
and choice of topic, 29, 52
adolescents, psychologically appropriate for, 75-80, 82
advantages of, 7
age of children and, 123-4, 126
allocation of tasks for, 2, 36, 45, 46, 51-2, 56
apparatus in, 32, 41, 56, 129-30
apprenticeship in, 20-1, 125, 127
approaches to, different, 44-7, 61-74, 123
attitudes in, development of new, 33-4, 39, 67, 73-4
children's reactions to, 1-11
children's responsibilities for, 5, 31, 33-4, 40, 99
children's self-direction in, *see* Group work, self-direction
children's suggestions for, 39, 43-4, 91
choice of topics, *see* Group work topics
conclusion of, 38, 64

Group Work—*continued*
confidence in, development of children's self-, 7, 32, 40-1
co-operation in, children's, 61-4, 79
cost of materials in, 32, 56, 126
covering the syllabus in, 4, 6, 38, 41, 57, **58**, 124-5, 129
critical attitude in, development of, 33-4, 39, 73-4
criticism in, development of self-, 30, 39, 74, 91, 93
criticisms of 6
definition of, working, 30
different approaches to, 44-7, 61-74, 123
direction in, self-, *see* Group work, self-direction in
discipline and, 116-18
discussion in, 4, 31-6, **43-4**, 45, 47, 55, 58, 70, 72, 80, 129
display in 23, 38, 45, 59, 60, 128, 131
division of labour in, 49, 51, 53; *see also* Allocation of tasks
dominating children in, 9, 53-4, 95, 120
drama in, 3, 5-6, 22, 24, 38, 41, 45, 46, 54, 59, 69
end-product of, 39, 40, 52, 54, 55, 60, 128; *see also* Group work, evaluation of
evaluation of, 24-5, 30, 40, 57-8, 113, 123-31
examinations and, 69-74, 82, 127
exhibitions in, 41, 59, 60, 69, 128
feasibility of schemes for, 44, 45, 65, 111, 128
flexibility of, 83
formal, 26
formation of groups for, *see* Groups, formation of
framework in, 2, 4, 5, 6, 42, 65, 83, 102, 103
freedom in, meaning of, 4-5, 124-5
freedom to pursue their own interests, children's, 3, 4, 5-6, 60, 67, 68, 70, 87, 125
ideas in, children's, 39, 43-4, 91
ideas in, teacher's, 31-6, 58, 110, 129
in action, 61-74
individual assignments in, 62-4
individual children, progress of, 57-8

individual contributions to, 61, 80
individual investigations in, 62-4
initiative in, children's, 7, 31, 38-9, 41
investigations in, children's, 2, 14, 61, 62
lesson periods needed for, number of **37-8**, 62-4, 70, 123, 126-7, 130
majority in, wishes of the, 3, 4, 36, 45, 55
materials for, 32, 36, 56-7, 126, 128
membership of groups in, *see* Groups, membership of
methods of, different, 44-7, 61-74, 123
mistakes in, children's, 32-3, 40, 52, 53
moods, suited to variations in children's, 79-80
nature of, 26-36, 41
not recommended as a universal method, viii, 10, 58, 115-16
organization of, 9-10, 20, 23, **37-60**, 61-74, 123, 126-8
personal involvement in, 67
plans for, 2-3, 5, 7, 20, 21, 23-4, 30, 31, **32-3**, 34, 37, 38, 40-1, **43-4**, 57, 62, 65, 66, 67
plays in, *see* Group work, drama in
preparation for, 36, 37; *see also* Group work, plans for
presentation of, 59-60, 62, 72; *see also* End-product of group work
principles of, 23, 26-36
problems of, 9, 44
procedure, 53-6
progress in, 30, 31, 34, 44, 56, 57-8
projects in, 1-2, 3-4, 5, 6, 8, 21-2, 24, 38, 41-7, 59, 63-4, 66, 68, 69-71, 72-4, 90, 125-6, 127; *see also* Projects suitable for Group work
questions in, use of, 30, 31, 40, 129
rationale of, 75-100
reactions to, children's, 1-11
reference books in, use of, 36, 57, 61-2
relevance of, 67-8
remedial classes and, 126, 127-8

Group Work—*continued*
  reporting back in, 2, 59-60
  responsibility for, children's, 5, 31, 33-4, 40, 99
  role of the teacher in, *see* Teacher, role of the
  schemes of, 20-2, 44; *see also* Group work, projects in
  school timetables and, **37-8**, 62-4, 65, 69, 70, 123, 126-7, 130
  self-confidence in, development of children's, 7, 32, 40-1
  self-criticism in, development of children's, 30, 39, 74, 91, 93
  self-direction in, children's, 4, **29-30**, 37, 51, 67, 80, 83-8
  skills in, use of children's, 51-2, 88, 124
  social behaviour, effects of, on, 69-70
  social education and, 75, 125
  sociometry in, 47-8
  sources of, 41-4
  speakers in, outside, 66, 67
  specifications for, 36, 38-44, 45, 47, 59
  standards of work in, 39, 42, 61, 62, 74
  students in, training of, *see* Students, training of
  success of, 36, 37, 38, 40, 41, 51, 53, 87, 123
  suggestions for, 20; children's, 39, 43-4, 91
  suggestions for, teacher's, 31-6, 58, 129
  supervision of students in, 2, 9, 21, 25, 105, 129-30
  syllabus in, coverage of, 4, 6, 38, 41, 57, **58**, 124-5, 129
  tasks in, allocation of, 2, 36, 45, 46, 51-2, 56
  teacher for, ultimate responsibility of the, 4-5, 30, 100
  teacher in, role of the, 5-6, 29, 30, **31-6**, 38, 40, 46, 53-7, 97-100, 118-21
  teacher inexperienced in, the, 33-5
  thematic, 21, 65-8, 126
  time needed for, 12, **37-8**, 62-4, 65, 123, 126-7, 130
  topics in, 1, 5, 21-2, 41-7, 49, 51, 53, 58, 59, 61, 62, 63, 64, 66, 71, 125-6; *see also* Topics in group work

  unused to, children, 5, 37, 38-9, 40-1, 59
  visits in, 56, 57, 63, 66, 70, 126
  voting in, 4, 36, 45, 55
  working parties in, 36, 45, 46
Groups, formation of, 8-9, 21, 26-8, 29, 30, 36, 37, 42, **44-53**, 72, 120
Groups, membership of, 9, 27, 47-53, 76-8, 90-100
Groups, peer-, 77, 79, 99, 100
Groups, reference, 76-7, 77n
Groups, size of, 21, 25, **49-50**, 52-3, 66, 127-8, 129
  of children, 21, 25, 49-50, 52-3, 66, 127-8, 129
  of students, 21, 127-8, 129
Groups, psychology of small, 23, 75-100
Groups, T-, 97-9
Groups, training, 97-8
Growth of Logical Thinking from Childhood to Adolescence, 82, 133

Hare, A. P., 88n, 133
Hawthorne experiments, 99
Health services, study of, 66-7
Herbart, J. F., 13
History, 63, 67, 125
Hobbies, children's, 43, 62, 88
Holidays, planning, 22, 41
  school, 127
Holt, John, 16, 133
Homework, 28
Hostility, children's, 13, 43, 91-2, 102; *see also* Aggression, children's
House management, 22
How Children Fail, 16, 133
Howard, John, 63
Hughes, Thomas, 84-5, 133

Ideas in competitive and co-operative discussions, students', 94-6
Ideas suggested by children, 39, 43-4, 91
  by teachers, 31-6, 58, 119, 129
In the Castle of My Skin, 86, 134
Incentives to learning, 13, 83-8, 94-6; *see also* Punishment
Individual assignments, 10, 14, 62-4
Individual children, progress of, 57-8
Individual contributions to discussion, assessment of, 94-6

Individual enterprise, 96
Individual, working as an, 2, 10, 14, 62-4, 80
Industriousness, children's, 91-3
Industry, 2, 16, 24, 56, 57, 70
    letters to firms, 2, 57, 70
    visits to firms 56, 57
Informal teaching methods, 20
Information, obtaining, 70-1
Inhelder, B., 82n, 13
Initiative, children's, 7, 31, 38-9, 41, 90, 96
Insecurity, children's feelings of, 4, 76-7; *see also* Security
Intellectual development, psychology of, 68, 74-5, 80-3
Interaction, group, 90-100; *see also* Groups, membership of
Inter-disciplinary inquiry, vii
Interest, children's lack of, 9, 13
Interests, children's 3, 4, 5-6, 29, 38, 41, **42-4**, 46, 51, 60, 61, 62, 67, 68, 70, 87, 125
    best starting-point for group work, 42, 67
    freedom to pursue, 3, 4, 5-6, 60, 67, 68, 70, 87, 125
    in choosing topics 29, 46, 61, 62
    in planning group work, 38, 41
    teacher's knowledge of, 43
Interests, teacher's, 41, 42-4, 46
Interior decorating, 41, 68, 69, 90
Investigation, children's, 2, 14, 61, 62
Involvement, high-activity, 92

Jackson, Brian, 27n, 134
Jaques, E., 98n, 134
Johnson, L. V., 100n, 132
Joint planning, *see* Group work, plans for
Juvenile delinquency, study of, 63
    potential, 24

Keate, Dr, 85
Knowledge, acquisition of, 55, 71, 74, 125
Knowledge, existence of a body of, 13, 15-7
Knowledge, gaps in, 6, 71; *see also*, Syllabus, coverage of

Laissez-faire methods, 53-5, 89-94
Lamming, George, 86, 134
Languages, 125
Law and order, project on, 3-4, 22

Laziness in children, 83, 91, 92
Leaders, group, 9, 53-5, 79, 87, 88-94
Learning, 8, 10, 13, 16-17, 27-8, 32-3, 35, 40, 52, 53, 80, 81, **83-8,** 94-6, 116
    by mistakes, 8, 32-3, 40, 52
    competition and co-operation in, 94-6
    incentives to, 13, 83-8, 94-6; *see also* Punishment
    through participation, 27-8, 35
Leicester, University of, 97-8
Lesson notes, 13; *see also* Logbook, students'
Lesson periods needed for group work, number of, 37-8, 62-4, 70, 123, 126-7, 130
Lesson planning, 61
Letters to firms, 2, 57, 70
Lewin, Kurt, 88n, 134
Libraries, use of, 2, 63
Lippitt, R., 53n, 88-94, 134, 136
Local studies, 21-2, 63, 72-4, 82
Locke, John, 83-4, 86, 134
Logbook, students', 23-4, 131
Logic, children's understanding of, 80-1
Lumsdaine, A. A., 134

Maccoby, E. E., 100n, 134
Machines, teaching, 33
Mackenzie, R. F., 14, 134
Magazines, school, 41
Majority, wishes of the, 3, 4, 36, 45, 55
Map-making, 22, 38, 41, 59, 72
Marionette theatre, production of a, 22
Marshall, Sybil, 60, 134
Materials for group work, 32, 36, 56-7, 126, 128
Mathematics, 67, 81, 125
Mayo, Elton, 99, 135
Medical services, 66
Membership groups, 76n
Membership of groups, *see* Groups
Memory, learning by rote, 16, 81
Mental development, psychology of, 68, 74-5, 80-3
Methods of teaching, 11, 20, 53-5, 89-94
    see also Group work
Mills, T. M., 98n, 135
Mistakes, learning by, 8, 32-3, 40, 52, 53

Mister Johnson, 54, 132
Mixed-ability classes, 20, 128
Mobile, construction of a, 22
Model-making, 1, 2, 38, 70, 90
Moods, children's, 79-80, 83-4
Moreno, J. L., 47, 135
Motor maintenance, 69

National Health Service, 66
National Training Laboratory in Group Development, Bethel, 97
'Newsom' children, 20, 130
Newsom Report, vii, 14, 133
Newspaper reading, survey of, 22
Newspapers, production of, 41, 56, 64, 67
Non-academic children, 14-15, 24
Non-streaming, vii
Notes, lesson, 13; *see also* Log-books, students'
Nuffield Foundation, vii, 115

Observation of teaching, 22, 104; *see also* Apprenticeship to group work
Occupations, survey of local, 72-4, 82
Oeser, O. A., 98, 135
Operations, logical, 80-1
Order in the classroom, 5
Organization of group work, *see* Group work, organization of
Ottaway, A. K. C., 98n, 135
Over-dependent children, 119
Oxfam, 66

Panel of students and tutors, 23
Paper, history of, 22
Parents, 77-9
Participation, 9, 27-8, 31-6, 58, 103, 119, 125, 129
Peer-groups, 77, 79, 99, 100
Personal involvement in group work, 67
Personal style in teaching, 10, 23, 26
Photography, 69
Physical development, 75-6
Piaget, Jean, 15, 80-3, 133
Pigeon-keeping, 63
Planes, project on, 8
Plans for group work, *see* Group work plans
Plato, 77, 85, 135
Plays in group work, *see* Drama

Plowden Committee, 86, 133
Postal services, survey of, 22
Power, project on, 1-2, 6, 22, 69-71
Practical difficulties of group work, 44
Praise, teacher's use of, 40, 89
Preliminary visits to schools, 128
Preparation for group work, 36, 37; *see also* Group work, plans for
Presentation of group work, 59-60, 62, 72; *see also* End-product of group work
Primary schools, 14, 81
Principles of group work, 23, 26-36
Problems of group work, 9, 44
Procedure, group, 53-6
Professional training, 12, 13
Projects, school, vii
Projects suitable for group work, 1-6, 8 ,21-2, 24, 38, 41-7, 59, 63-4, 66, 68, 69-71, 72-4, 90, 125-6, 127
building, 22, 41, 69
camps, school, 127
canoeing, 69
chickens, keeping, 63
climbing, 68, 69
concerts, 41
decorating, interior, 41, 68, 69, 90
electricity, 1, 22, 70-1
employment, investigation into, 63-4, 72-4
film-making, 38, 41
health services, 66
holidays, planning, 22, 41
law and order, 3-4, 22
local studies, 21-2, 63-4, 72-4
magazines, school, 41
map-making, 22, 38, 41, 59, 72
marionette theatre, production of a, 22
masques, 41, 59
mobile, construction of a, 22
model-making, 1, 2, 38, 70, 90
motor maintenance, 69
newspaper reading, survey of, 22
newspapers, production of, 41, 56, 64, 67
occupations, survey of local, 72-4, 82
operas, 41
Oxfam, appeal for, 66
pageants, 41
photography, 69
pigeon-keeping, 63

144 *Index*

Projects—*continued*
  planes, 8
  police, 3
  postal services, survey of, 22
  power, 1-2, 6, 22, 69-71
  rivers, 22
  social services, study of, 22, 41
  surveys, 22, 41, 59, 72-4
  swimming, 69
  telephones, 22, 24
  workshop, building and engineering, 22
  see also Group work topics
Psychological experiments, observation of, 90
Psychological weaning, 77, 79, 99
Psychology, child, 12, 80
Psychology of adolescence and puberty, 68, 75-83, 96, 99-100
Psychology, social, 88-100
Puberty, 75-80
Public speaking, 8
Punishment, 7, 13, 68, 80, 81, 83-8

Questions, teacher's use of, 30, 31, 40, 129

Radio broadcasts, use of, 63, 67
Rationale of group work, 75-100
Reactions to group work, children's, 1-11
Rebelliousness, children's, 51, 68-9, 77, 78, 79, 99
Recognition, need for, 98-100
Records in group work, keeping, 23-4, 34, 36, 56, **57-8**, 59, 131
  children's, 34, 36, 56, 57-8, 59
  students' logbooks, 23-4, 131
  teachers', 57-8
Reference books, use of, 36, 57, 61-2
Reference groups, 76-7, 77n
Rejection of each other, children's, *see* Groups, formation of
Relevance of group work, 67-8
Remedial classes, 126, 127-8
Reporting back in group work, 2, 59-60
Responsibility for their work, children's, 5, 31, 33-4, 40, 99
Responsibility, the teacher's, 4-5, 30, 118
Rewarding argument, self-, 83, 87-8
Rewards, 7, 13, 81; *see also* Punishment
Richardson, J. L., 93, 135
River, study of a, 22

Rote memory, learning by, 16, 81
Rowe, A. D., 14, 135
Rural science, 67

Sacred Band of Thebes, 77
Safety, children's, 30
Schemes of group work, 20-2, 44; *see also* Group work projects
School administration, 20, 41, 123
  and organization of group work, 20
School timetables, 12, **37-8**, 62-4, 65, 69, 70, 123, 126-7, 130
School-leaving age raising the, 15
Schools, 10-11, 12, 14, 15, 16, 17, 19-25, 68, 81, 101-14, 123-31
  comprehensive, 15, 68
  grammar, 12, 15, 16, 17
  middle, 109
  primary, 14, 81
  progressive, 14
  public, 12
  secondary modern, 14
Schools and colleges, co-operation between, 10-11, 19-25, 101-14, 123-31
Schools Council, 15, 135
Schools for teaching practice, use of, 19
Science, 67
Secondary training, students' reasons for, 12
Security, children's feelings of, 4, 76-7, 96, 119
Self-analysis, students', 107
Self-confidence, development of children's, 5, 7, 32, 40-1, 76
Self-control, 83
Self-criticism, development of, 30, 39, 74, 91, 93
Self-direction, children's, 4, 29-30, 37, 51, 67, 80, 83-8
Self-expression, children's, 7
Self-rewarding argument, 83, 87-8
Self-selected groups, *see* Groups, formation of
Sensory experience, 8-1, 82, 97
Sherif, M. & C. W., 77n, 135
Size of groups, 21, 25, **49-50**, 52-3, 66, 127-8, 129
Skills, children's 51-2, 88, 124
Skinner, B. F., 86, 135
Slow children, 8
Small groups, psychology of, 23, 75-100
Social behaviour, children's, 68-9

Social education, 75, 125
Social psychology, 88-100
Social services, 22, 41, 66
Sociograms, 47
Sociology, educational, 12
Sociometry, 47-8, 50, 88
Sources of group work, 41-4
South Africa, 27n
Speakers, outside, 66, 67
Specifications for group work, 36, 38-44, 45, 47, 59
Standards of work, 39, 42, 61, 62, 74
Steiner, Rudolf, 84, 135
Storage, 128
Strang, Ruth, viii n, 136
Streaming, vii, 27
Students, training of, 2, 9, 10, **12-25**, 26, 98, **101-14**, 123-31
in group-work methods, 12-25, 26, 98, 101-14, 123-31
teaching practice in, 19, 20, 22, 25, 26, 124
topics, students', 105, 106, 111
supervision of, 2, 9, 10, 21, 23, 25, 105, 106, 129-30
Subjects in group work, curriculum, 21, 22, 63, 65, 67, 68, 69, 71, 81, 125
Art, 69
English, 125
Geography, 63, 67, 71
Geometry, 22
History, 63, 67, 125
Languages, 125
Mathematics, 67, 81, 125
Science, 67
Subject-teaching, 12-17; *see also* Teacher-directed lessons
Submissive children, 69, 79, 91-2, 119
Success of group work, 36, 37, 38, 40, 41, 51, 53, 87, 123
Suggestions, children's, 39, 43-4, 91 teachers', 31-6, 58, 129
Supervision, children's need of, 90-3
Supervision of students, 2, 7, 9, 10, 21, 23, 25, 105, 106, **129-30**
Surveys, 22, 41, 59, 72-4
Syllabus, coverage of, 4, 6, 38, 41, 57, **58**, 71, 124-5, 129
Sympathetic understanding of children, need for, 9-10
Symposium, 77, 135

Tanner, J. M., 78, 136

Tavistock Institute, 97, 98n
Teacher, authority of the, 4-5, 12-13, 68, 84, 97, 99, 123
Teacher, defiance of the, 68-9, 77-8, 80; *see also* Rebelliousness, children's
Teacher, responsibility of the, 4-5, 30, 100, 118
Teacher, role of the, 5-6, 20-1, 27-8, 29, 30, 31-6, 38, 40-4, 46, 53-7, 97-100, 104-6, 118-21, 129-30
in group work, 5-6, 29, 30, **31-6**, 38, 40, 46, 53-7, 97-100, 118-21
in teacher-directed lessons, 27-8, 30
in training students in group work, 20-1, 104-6, 129-30
Teacher, skill of the, 38-9, 42-3, 116, 120
Teacher-directed lessons, traditional, vii, 4, 7, 10, 13-17, 23, **27-8**, 30, 39, 51, 58, 62, 69, 71, 75, 101, 102
class teaching in, vii, 4, 51, 58, 62
restrictions of, 4, 35, 71
role of the teacher in, 27-8, 30
transition from, 61, 62-3
Teachers and college tutors, cooperation between, 10-11, 19-25, 101-14, 123-31
Teachers, secondary, vii, 12-14
Teacher's use of blame, 89
of praise, 40, 89
of questions, 30, 31, 40, 129
Teaching a personal art, 10, 23, 26
Teaching, group, 26-30
Teaching, ingredients of good, 9-10
Teaching machines, 33
Teaching practice, 19, 20, 22, 25, 26, 124
Team teaching, vii, 10, 124
Technological change, 14, 16
Telephone, study of the, 22, 24
Television, use of, 63, 64, 67
Temperamental differences, 79-80, 83-4
Terms suitable for group work, school, 127
Textbooks, use of, 28, 61-2
copying from, 61-2
T-groups, 97-8
Thelen, H. A., vii n, 98, 136
Thematic group work, 21, 65-8, 126
Timber, study of, 22
Time needed for group work, 12, **37-8**, 62-4, 65, 123, 126-7, 130

Timetables, school, *see* School timetables
Tom Brown's Schooldays, 84-5, 86, 133
Topic work, 14
Topics in group work, 1, 5, 21-2, 41-7, 49, 51, 53, 58, 59, 61, 62, 63, 64, 66, 71, 125-6
  budgeting, 22
  foodstuffs, 66
  health services, 66-7
  house management, 22
  insurance, 66
  medical services, 66
  paper, history of, 22
  pensions, 66
  popularity of, 49, 51, 53
  prison reform, 63
  teacher's ideas for, 64, 71
  trees, 22
  written word, history of the, 22
  see also Group work, projects in
Topics in the training of students, 105, 106, 111
Traditional class teaching, *see* Teacher-directed lessons
Training groups, 97-8
Training, professional, 12-13
Transport, arrangements for, 56, 130
Trees, study of, 22
Troublemakers, 51

Tutors, co-operation between teachers and college, 10-11, 19-25, 101-14, 123-31

U.N.I.C.E.F., 66
Understanding contrasted with rote learning, 16-17, 81
Understanding of children, need for sympathetic, 9-10
University departments of education, 12
Unpopular children, 50

Visits, school, 56, 57, 63, 70, 126, 130
Voss, 59, 133
Voting, 4, 36, 45, 55; *see also* Majority, wishes of the

Watson, G., 136
White, Patrick, 59, 133
White, R. K., 53n, 88-94, 134, 136
Wilmott, Peter, 77n, 136
Work parties, 14
Working parties in group work, 36, 45, 46
Workshop, building and engineering, 22

Yates, A., 27n, 136

Zander, A., 100n, 132